SECOND EDITION

Practical Suggestions for Teaching *Real Skills*

Eddye S. Gallagher
Tarrant County College

BEDFORD/ST. MARTIN'S

Boston ◆ New York

Manufactured in the United States of America.
5 4 3 2 1 0
f e d c b a
For information, write: Bedford/St. Martin's, 75 Arlington Street, Boston, MA 02116
(617-399-4000)

ISBN-10: 0–312–56716–2
ISBN-13: 978–0–312–56716–3

Instructors who have adopted *Real Skills*, Second Edition, as a textbook for a course
are authorized to duplicate portions of this manual for their students.

Contents

1

How to Use Real Skills *in Your Course*

Welcome to *Real Skills*, and (if you are a new instructor) welcome to developmental writing instruction. This instructor's manual will, I hope, give you some practical ideas for using *Real Skills* and its support materials as aids to understanding and helping your students, teaching the course, and facing the challenges of our profession.

This chapter starts with first things first: what to do the very first day you walk into the class with *Real Skills* in your hands and a collection of new students in front of you. After that come overviews of *Real Skills* and its ancillary package, and some sample syllabi and class schedules that demonstrate how to integrate *Real Skills* into the course.

Susan Anker, the editors at Bedford/St. Martin's, the contributing authors, and I have tried to make this instructor's manual and the other parts of *Real Skills* as helpful to you as possible. We are interested in hearing your feedback, particularly if you have ideas about how to improve the coverage or make it more useful. Please write to us at *Real Skills*, Bedford/St. Martin's, 75 Arlington Street, Boston, MA 02116.

What to Do on Day One

The first day of class can set the tone for the entire semester, so prepare yourself and your plans carefully. If you approach the day with a great attitude and a smile on your face, your students will probably be quite receptive to you and your course. How much you can accomplish during the first day will depend on the length of your class, the promptness of your students, and your own preparedness.

PREPARATION. Before class, read through this chapter of *Practical Suggestions;* if you are a new instructor, also read Chapter 2, Tips for New Instructors, and Chapter 3, Working with Developmental Writers. If you have time, read the preface in *Real Skills* to acquaint yourself with the book and its features; skim through Chapter 1 of *Real Skills* if you intend to assign that chapter or go over it in class. Plan out the activities you want to cover on the first day, figuring out approximately how much time you will spend on each activity. (It is better to plan too much than too little.) Bring your copy of *Real Skills* and samples of any supplies that you will want students to have (three-ring notebooks, computer disks, pens, and so on). Also, prepare any of the following handouts to distribute to your students:

- Student Information Form (sample on p. 3)

- Syllabus (sample on p. 7)

- List of required texts and supplies

- Grading policy

- Attendance policy

- Class schedules or assignment schedules (samples on pp. 13–18)

- Acknowledgment of Student Responsibilities (sample on p. 27)

- Critical thinking activities to use as icebreakers (samples on pp. 59–73)

Arrive at the classroom early so that you can write important information on the board; this aid gives ESL or other students a head start and saves time for other activities. Greet your students as they come into the room.

INTRODUCTIONS. Begin the class by welcoming your students to the course and introducing yourself. Yes, your name may be on their class schedules, but saying it lets students know how to pronounce it and reinforces your identity. I also stress the importance names have for all of us. As I begin to call roll, I say, "Please let me know if I'm mispronouncing your name or calling you something that you prefer not to be called." If a student's name is particularly hard for me to pronounce, I ask the student to bear with me as I learn the pronunciation and to remind me if I forget.

OVERVIEW. After roll call, you may want to give a brief course overview. You can distribute the course syllabus and class schedule (see pp. 7, 13–18 for samples) and discuss student responsibilities, course focus, the grading system, and text and supply requirements. I would not go into a tremendous amount of detail. Basically, just walk your students through the syllabus, pointing out various sections of particular importance. You could even make reading the syllabus a homework assignment for the next class. Keep the presentation very short. You will discover that students will forget much of what you say on the first day; therefore, you will need to repeat some information during another class period. Although many students will not retain the introductory information, most will appreciate knowing from the beginning what to expect. Every few minutes throughout class, ask for questions. Although you may get few, if any, you are at least establishing that you encourage questions.

LOGISTICS. When introducing necessary supplies, follow the same guidelines—keep the discussion short and ask if students have questions. Have your textbooks handy and hold them up as you refer to them. If you use more than one, you might want to mention how each will be used. This is a great time to explain whether students will need to bring supplies for computer work. Also, point out any special paper restrictions that you have about materials. Your students want to please you, so give them a warning if you have pet peeves about certain supplies. (For example, I cannot stand colored or spiral-bound paper.) To help keep your students organized, ask them to purchase a three-ring binder to hold all of their class assignments and writings. Explicitly tell your class how you want the binder organized and maintained.

ENCOURAGEMENT AND RAPPORT. You will probably want to give a pep talk about how much the students can learn during the semester and how you are going to be their guide to success. In my school, students receive no credit for developmental courses, so I usually emphasize the benefits the course will provide as they move into the credit (and graded) classes. I tell them that the composition teachers love to get students from the developmental writing classes because those students are well prepared, ready to work, and not afraid to write. I want them to see the connection between my class and their success in other classes (not just English), their careers, and their everyday lives.

Try to establish a feeling of comfort and openness from day one. My students (and perhaps yours also) enter the course through various avenues: a low score on the state exam or the college's placement test, their own recognition of their weaknesses in grammar and/or writing, or the recommendation of a counselor or another teacher. Those who have not passed the placement tests sometimes resent having to be in my class, so I discuss why they "may" have entered the class. I even mention negative attitudes they have because of low test scores or previous failures in English classes. Then I say, "But, let's put all of that aside now. We're all here together, so let's establish goals for the semester. Do you want to improve your grammar skills, develop strong thesis statements, learn how to gather research, and write coherent essays? Let's focus on what you want to accomplish this semester and how we are going to work together to reach your goals. I'm not going to tell you how you must write, but I will offer suggestions to make the writing process easier for you. I don't expect you all to leave my class saying, 'I love to write; I love English,' but if I can get you to say, 'Oh, the semester was okay; writing's not too bad,' then I will have succeeded and you will have made a giant step toward reaching your goals." I also stress that the class is designed to help students learn and improve, and that no one in the class should be afraid of making mistakes—which, of course, is often a means of learning.

Student Information Form

Name: _____   Class Time: _____

Address: _____   Phone: _____

_____   E-mail: _____

Other Courses Currently Taking:

_____

_____

_____

Current Employment: _____

Work Schedule: _____

Have you taken this class before? _____

If yes, when? _____

Is there anything about you that I need to know in order to help you do your best this semester?

_____

_____

_____

_____

_____

_____

_____

_____

BASIC INFORMATION. You may want to ask students to complete the Student Information Form on page 3. You can also ask for pertinent information that will help you help them: learning preferences, travel requirements for work, and so on. I usually say, "Tell me anything about yourself that might prevent your 100 percent effort in this class, such as being the single parent of ten kids." Giving such an exaggerated example can help students feel comfortable revealing personal information.

REAL SKILLS. Ask students to familiarize themselves with their textbooks and let them know how important *Real Skills* is to their success in the class, to the improvement of their writing, and to their careers (both in college and at work) outside your classroom. Consider assigning *Real Skills'* student introduction to be read before the next class meeting. (You can discuss the introduction in class to ensure that students have completed this assignment.) The introduction orients students to the organization and features of *Real Skills*. Many developmental students are unfamiliar with the characteristics of textbooks and do not know how to use them effectively, so they will benefit from this overview.

ICEBREAKERS. A critical thinking activity from Chapter 5 of this manual could serve as a great icebreaker. Or, you can try one of these:

- Ask students to line themselves up by a specific characteristic: alphabetically by last name, by place of birth, by academic major, or by birthday. They will inevitably introduce themselves and learn about each other as they figure out the correct order in which to line up.

- Have students pair up to interview each other. Then, they should introduce each other to the class.

- Conduct a scavenger hunt for people in the class. Divide the students into groups and give each group a list of people to find: the person who has read the most books in the last three months; someone who grew up in the town the college is in; anyone born in a foreign country.

WRITING SAMPLE. Students need to begin thinking of themselves as writers, and you need to get samples of their writing so that you can assess their needs; it is therefore important to have them do some actual writing on the first day of class. Ask them to write a sample paragraph. I like to ask students to describe the best or worst English class they have ever taken: Most students have experienced either a good or a bad class, so they have content to impart, and their descriptions tell me a great deal about their attitudes and expectations. You may want to end the class period with the request for the writing sample so that those who write slowly will not feel pressured and those who write quickly can leave when they finish.

CLOSURE. End the class by reemphasizing your positive attitude toward the semester and by making an assignment for the second class. You can make the assignment as simple as reading the syllabus/class schedule and purchasing texts and supplies, or you can jump right into a reading assignment from *Real Skills*. You can see the sample class schedules starting on page 13 for suggested assignments during the first week. Also encourage students to call you, or e-mail you, or come by your office if they have questions or to jot down the questions to ask at the next class. As you dismiss the class, tell them to have a nice day (or evening) and cheerfully call out, "I'll see you next class!"

THE REST OF THE FIRST WEEK. During the rest of the first week of class, make sure you accomplish any of the goals that you were not able to fit in on the first day. In addition, give students a diagnostic grammar test so that you can assess their needs both as individuals and as a class. (See *Additional Resources* for pre- and post-tests. Diagnostic tests are also available on the *Testing Tool Kit* CD with this book.) If you are going to be teaching in a computer lab or otherwise requiring the use of computers, build in time for acquainting students with the computer-related logistics. Also, talk about other resources on campus, such as the writing center or library; you may even want to plan a visit. Finally, you may want to discuss plagiarism and give your students a written statement (such as the one found in Chapter 2 of this book) to clarify both the concept and its consequences. See also the tutorial on avoiding plagiarism at **bedfordstmartins.com/rewriting**.

Overview of *Real Skills*

Real Skills is organized to be both straightforward and flexible. Part 1 of the book serves as a kind of introduction to college, with advice from former students on staying in college (Chapter 1) and on succeeding academically by managing time, improving reading skills, preparing for tests, and so on (Chapter 2). Chapter 3 of the first part includes a questionnaire to help students find their predominant learning style(s). It then lists features in the book that help students take advantage of their learning preferences, including numerous collaborative activities (labeled "Practice Together"). Part 2 begins with an overview of the basics of good writing and then gives detailed advice on the process of writing paragraphs. The final chapter of Part 2 helps students move from paragraphs to essays. Parts 3–7 provide detailed coverage—with plenty of examples and practices—of grammar, style, punctuation, and mechanics. Included in these parts are many "Find and Fix" and chapter review charts to help students find and edit errors on their own. Parts 2–7 end with tests that help you gauge students' mastery of writing and grammar skills. Part 8 is a collection of readings that can be used as models or to spark writing.

It might be helpful to begin the course with Part 1, which serves as a great introduction and helps build students' confidence. Then, you might want to use one or more of the writing-process chapters (4–7) before assigning one or more of the paragraphs from Chapter 8, or assignments of your own. (The paragraph coverage in Chapter 8 is organized according to the various rhetorical strategies.) Toward the end of the class, you might want to introduce students to the essay (Chapter 9).

Different instructors have different ways of integrating grammar instruction. Consider assigning Chapter 10, The Complete Sentence: Key Parts to Know, early in the semester; it is an excellent review of the basics and should help allay some students' fears about grammar. *Real Skills* emphasizes the four most serious errors (fragments, run-ons and comma splices, problems with subject-verb agreement, and problems with verb tense), so you may want to assign the chapters that address these errors (in Part 3) to the whole class and discuss them during class. You can assign other grammar chapters as needed, either to individuals or to the entire class.

Part 8, the readings, is organized according to rhetorical strategy, which should make it easy for you to integrate the selections into your class and to connect reading with writing. When students are working on their process analysis paragraphs, for example, you can easily direct them to the professional examples in Chapter 37.

Real Skills is filled with features designed to make the course useful to your students and to help them become better writers. I recommend reading through the first few pages of the *Instructor's Annotated Edition of Real Skills* and the preface to give yourself an overview of these features.

Sample Syllabus and Class Schedules

As I am using the terms, a *syllabus* is a written description of a course's content, requirements, and policies, whereas a *class schedule* outlines what work is to be completed each day or week during the semester. Regardless of what terminology you use, I hope the following examples will be useful to you.

Sample Syllabus

Your school's or state's requirements may determine how much information you need to include in the syllabus that you distribute to your students. As a minimum, you will probably want to include a course description, a statement of attendance and grading policies, a list of required texts and supplies, and an explanation of available resources. The syllabus on pages 7–10 is an example that might be helpful.

Developmental English Course Syllabus

INSTRUCTOR:

OFFICE:

OFFICE HOURS:

PHONE:

E-MAIL:

Course Description

Developmental English is a basic writing course designed to prepare you for Freshman Composition.

Course Focus

The course focuses on principles of grammar, usage, sentence structure, and paragraph development.

Texts and References

Anker, Susan. *Real Skills*. 2nd ed. Boston: Bedford/St. Martin's, 2010.
A college dictionary.

Course Goals

Classes will have some lecture, discussion, and media presentations. In addition, during some classes, you will write and revise your assignments. The course covers the following content goals, although sequence may vary.

   A. Usage and Mechanics
         1. Use nouns and pronouns correctly as subjects or objects.
         2. Use correct verb forms.
         3. Use modifiers effectively in a sentence.
         4. Identify unnecessary shifts in verb tense.
         5. Identify shifts in person.
         6. Display standard punctuation and capitalization skills.
         7. Display standard spelling skills.
         8. Complete classroom and/or laboratory assignments.
   B. Sentence Structure
         1. Write clear and correct sentences.
         2. Write parallel sentence structures.
         3. Correct comma splices or run-ons.
         4. Correct sentence fragments.
         5. Demonstrate understanding of subject-verb agreement.
         6. Write sentences that combine ideas correctly.
   C. Unity and Focus
         1. Select writing topics.
         2. Practice prewriting strategies.
         3. Focus writing topics.
         4. Distinguish between effective and ineffective topic sentences.
         5. Formulate topic sentences.
         6. Demonstrate use of appropriate transitional words and phrases.

D. Organization and Development
1. Identify a paragraph's topic sentence.
2. Identify a paragraph's support points.
3. Identify a paragraph's concluding sentence.
4. Identify methods of ordering ideas in a paragraph.
5. Outline paragraph content.
6. Convert outlines into paragraphs.
7. Write different kinds of paragraphs (e.g., narration, illustration, cause/effect, argument, etc.).
8. Develop ideas and arguments.
9. Learn the differences between paragraphs and essays and know how to write an essay.
E. Appropriateness
1. Identify writing purpose.
2. Identify audience.
3. Demonstrate appropriate and varied word choice.
4. Demonstrate appropriate personal style and voice.
5. Proofread your work.
F. Exit Skills
1. Complete timed in-class writings.
2. Complete final writing sample.

Student Contributions

1. You need to spend at least six hours per week preparing for class. Timely completion of class work and home assignments is crucial.

2. If you need additional computer time to work on your papers, you may visit the Writing Center or the Computer Learning Center.

3. You can also improve your reading and writing skills through independent study in the Learning Mall or Computer Learning Center and conferences with your instructor.

4. You should attend class regularly because major concepts are explained in class and much of the writing and daily work will be done in class.

5. If you miss roll call because you are tardy, contact the instructor as soon as class is over, or you will be counted absent.

6. If absent, you are responsible for discovering what you missed and for preparing assignments for the next class. Makeup work is allowed only at the instructor's discretion.

7. Complete and submit course work by specified deadlines. Papers turned in after the due date will not receive full credit. Your absence from class on the day an assignment is due does not excuse the assignment from being late. If the instructor approves, some late work may be made up by a specified deadline.

8. If you must withdraw from this course, you are responsible for contacting the registrar.

Course Evaluation

The final grade will be *credit* or *no credit*. To receive credit, you must make an average of at least 70 in the course and complete a timed essay at the end of the semester.

Your semester grade will be based on the following:

Homework, in-class activities	10%
Spelling tests + comprehensive final	10%
Part tests on mechanics, usage, sentence structure + comprehensive final	30%
Essay assignments	40%
Final writing exam (timed)	10%

Performance Objectives

Your mastery of the performance objectives will be evaluated in several ways, with a score of 70 considered mastery. Your recall of text assignments, laboratory practice, lecture notes, and class assignments will be tested according to each instructor's directions. Your responses must be consistent with the text and lectures. Individual instructors may emphasize, in a personal manner, course content, order, and related topics. Writing assignments are also a critical part of demonstrating mastery of the performance objectives. Performance will be satisfactory if these skills are practiced and applied in your paragraphs and essays. To show mastery of course goals, you will be required to

1. Write sentences that demonstrate correct usage of the parts of speech, punctuation, and capitalization.

2. Demonstrate precision and variety in choice of words.

3. Write sentences, paragraphs, and essays free of sentence errors.

4. Write sentences, paragraphs, and essays free of shifts in person and errors in verb tense.

5. Determine the audience and purpose of a paragraph or essay.

6. Demonstrate the ability to write a clear focus statement for both a paragraph and an essay.

7. Demonstrate the ability to develop ideas and arguments in appropriate order to produce a well-developed, unified, coherent paragraph and/or essay.

8. Demonstrate the ability to proofread and revise paragraphs and essays.

9. Complete the timed writing. Performance will be satisfactory if the writing sample effectively communicates a whole message to the specified audience for the stated purpose and you score 70 percent correct on the objective test.

Special Instructions

A. *Materials*

You will need the following supplies for this course:
- 8½" x 11" white, lined loose-leaf notebook paper
- SCAN-TRON Sheets (Form 882ES)
- Three-ring loose-leaf binder
- Blue or black ink pens, no. 2 pencils
- Colored pens for editing (ballpoint pen and highlighter)
- Two writeable CDs
- Protective carrying case for CDs

B. *Special Help or Instruction*

Several areas are available for assistance with special problems and your assignments. Some areas will require you to show a current student ID.

The Skills Center, located in ACB 109, is open 7:30 a.m. to 10:00 p.m. (M–Th) and 7:30 a.m. to 5:00 p.m. (F) during the long terms, and 7:30 a.m. to 9:00 p.m. (M–Th) during the summer. Sometimes you will have a required assignment that uses the center's materials; therefore, it is important that you arrange your schedule so that you can use this learning facility.

Also located in ACB 109, *The Writing Center* operates from 7:30 a.m. to 9:30 p.m. (M–Th) and 7:30 a.m. to 4:30 p.m. (F) during long terms only. An English consultant is available to help you understand your assignments and improve your writing skills. The area also has Macintosh computers available for your use.

The Computer Learning Center, located in LRC 101, is open from 7:45 a.m. to 9:45 p.m. (M–Th), 7:45 a.m. to 4:45 p.m. (F), and 7:45 a.m. to 3 p.m. (Sat) during long terms. Summer hours are 7:30 a.m. to 10 p.m. (M–Th). You can work on your own as you see a need, or your instructor may assign you a specific software program to complete. The CLC personnel are trained to assist you with the computers.

Sample Class Schedules

Whether or not you distribute a class schedule to your students, you will probably want to create one for your own use. Always plan more than you think you can cover. Doing so can prevent the embarrassment of not knowing what to do with extra time; besides, eliminating assignments rather than adding assignments can enhance your reputation with your students.

The two sample schedules included here model different configurations based on different numbers of weeks. These schedules can easily be adapted for use in a computer classroom or lab by setting aside one day during the first week to introduce students to the computers and one day during the second week for an introduction to the word processing software. Allow students to plan and/or draft some of their writing at home and then use class time for typing the assignment into the computer, editing, and revising. In addition, you can substitute appropriate chapters when you have determined the type of grammar, sentence structure, word usage, and punctuation assistance your students need. Furthermore, if your school or state requires an exit essay, you may want to include two or three in-class paragraphs or essays and concentrate on the particular rhetorical mode or modes in which your students will be required to write.

Class Schedule for a 16-Week Course

Note: This class schedule focuses on six modes of writing: narration, illustration, description, process analysis, cause and effect, and argument. Relevant readings can be assigned as needed from Part 8 of Real Skills.

Week One
Reading Assignment: Ch. 1, Staying in College: Advice from Those Who Have Been There. Ch. 2, Doing Well in College: Strategies for Success. Ch. 4, Understanding the Basics of Good Writing: How to Write in College and Other Formal Settings.

Classroom Activities: Introduction to course. Student Introduction to *Real Skills*. In-class diagnostic writing. In-class diagnostic grammar test. Learning-styles survey. Overview of the writing process.

Writing Assignment: Paragraph on steps students could take to stay in college.

Week Two
Reading Assignment: Ch. 5, Narrowing and Exploring Your Topic: How to Decide What to Write About. Narration and illustration coverage in Ch. 8, Developing Your Paragraph: Different Ways to Present Your Ideas. Ch. 10, The Complete Sentence: Key Parts to Know.

Classroom Activities: Practice choosing topics and prewriting. Review homework exercises.

Writing Assignment: Find and explore topics for narration and illustration paragraphs.

Week Three
Reading Assignment: Ch. 6, Writing Your Paragraph: How to Put Your Ideas Together. Ch. 11, Fragments: Sentences That Are Missing a Key Part.

Classroom Activities: Group work on effective topic sentences and specific details (see Practice Together activities in Chapter 6). Review homework exercises.

Writing Assignment: Write topic sentences for narration and illustration paragraphs. Find supporting details, examples, and facts.

Week Four
Reading Assignment: Description and process analysis coverage in Ch. 8, Developing Your Paragraph: Different Ways to Present Your Ideas. Ch. 12, Run-Ons: Two Sentences Joined Incorrectly.

Classroom Activities: Work on ordering details in narration and illustration paragraphs. Do group activities (Practice Together) in Chapters 8 and/or 12. Review homework exercises.

Writing Assignment: Finish arranging details for narration and illustration paragraphs. Begin prewriting and narrowing ideas for description and process analysis paragraphs.

Week Five
Reading Assignment: Ch. 13, Subject-Verb Agreement Problems: Subjects and Verbs That Do Not Match. Ch. 14, Verbs: The Past Tense.

Classroom Activities: Begin writing topic sentences for description and process analysis paragraphs and selecting supporting details. Do group activities (Practice Together) in Chapters 13 and/or 14. Review homework exercises.

Writing Assignment: Draft narration and illustration paragraphs.

Week Six

Reading Assignment: Ch. 7, Improving Your Paragraph: How to Make It the Best It Can Be. Ch. 15, Verbs: The Past Participle.

Classroom Activities: Arrange details for description and process analysis paragraphs. Introduce peer evaluation and have students review each other's narration and illustration drafts. Do group activities (Practice Together) in Chapters 7 and/or 15. Review homework exercises.

Writing Assignment: Revise narration and illustration paragraphs. Draft description and process analysis paragraphs.

Week Seven

Reading Assignment: Cause-and-effect and argument coverage in Ch. 8, Developing Your Paragraph: Different Ways to Present Your Ideas. Ch. 16, Nouns: Using Plural Forms. Ch. 17, Pronouns: Using Substitutes for Nouns.

Classroom Activities: Narrowing and prewriting for cause-and-effect and argument topics. Peer review of description and process analysis paragraphs. Do group activities (Practice Together) in Chapters 16 and/or 17. Review homework exercises.

Writing Assignment: Revise description and process analysis paragraphs. Work on writing topic sentences and choosing and arranging details for cause-and-effect and argument paragraphs.

Week Eight

Reading Assignment: Ch. 18, Adjectives and Adverbs: Describing *Which One?* or *How?* Ch. 19, Misplaced and Dangling Modifiers: Avoiding Confusing Descriptions.

Classroom Activities: Conferences with students on their progress. Answer questions about and provide assistance with cause-and-effect and argument paragraphs. Meanwhile, other students can work on drafting these paragraphs. Review homework exercises.

Writing Assignment: Journal entry on what students have learned so far. Finish cause-and-effect and argument paragraph drafts.

Week Nine

Reading Assignment: Ch. 20, Illogical Shifts: Avoiding Inconsistencies. Ch. 22, Coordination: Joining Sentences with Related Ideas. Ch. 23, Subordination: Joining Sentences with Related Ideas.

Classroom Activities: Peer review of cause-and-effect and argument paragraphs. Do group activities (Practice Together) in Chapter 20, 22, or 23. Review homework exercises.

Writing Assignment: Revise cause-and-effect and argument paragraphs.

Week Ten

Reading Assignment: Ch. 24, Parallelism: Balancing Ideas. Ch. 25, Word Choice: Using the Right Words.

Classroom Activities: Do group activities (Practice Together) in Chapters 24 and/or 25. Review homework exercises.

Writing Assignment: Do an additional revision of two paragraphs previously completed.

Week Eleven

Reading Assignment: Ch. 9, Moving from Paragraphs to Essays: How to Write Longer Papers. Ch. 26, Commonly Confused Words: Choosing the Right Word When It Sounds Like Another Word.

Classroom Activities: Discuss the differences between paragraphs and essays. Assign or ask students to pick an essay topic. Do group activities (Practice Together) in Chapters 9 and/or 26. Review homework exercises.

Writing Assignment: Prewriting for essay topic.

Week Twelve

Reading Assignment: Ch. 27, Spelling: Using the Right Letters. Ch. 28, Commas.

Classroom Activities: Peer review of prewriting for essay topics. Students should help each other expand support for essays. Do group activities (Practice Together) in Chapters 27 and/or 28. Review homework exercises.

Writing Assignment: Write thesis statement for essay and arrange supporting points into an outline.

Week Thirteen

Reading Assignment: Ch. 29, Apostrophes. Ch. 30, Quotation Marks.

Classroom Activities: Vocabulary games (see Appendix B, Building Your Vocabulary). Do group activities (Practice Together) in Chapters 29 and/or 30. Review homework exercises.

Writing Assignment: Draft essay.

Week Fourteen

Reading Assignment: Ch. 31, Other Punctuation.

Classroom Activities: Peer review of draft essay. Do group activities (Practice Together) in Chapter 31. Review homework exercises.

Writing Assignment: Revise draft essay.

Week Fifteen

Reading Assignment: Appendix A, Succeeding on Tests. Ch. 32, Capitalization: Using Capital Letters.

Classroom Activities: Answer questions about final exam. Do group activities (Practice Together) in Chapter 32. Review homework exercises.

Writing Assignment: None. Suggest that students use the time to study for the final exam and to time themselves on a sample writing for the writing exam. Consider giving them practice topics to work with.

Week Sixteen

Classroom Activities: Final preparation for, and completion of, final.

Writing Assignment: In-class writing final. Final grammar test.

Class Schedule for a 10-Week Course

Note: This class schedule focuses on four modes of writing: narration, illustration, comparison and contrast, and argument. Relevant readings can be assigned as needed from Part 8 of Real Skills.

Week One

Reading Assignment: Ch. 1, Staying in College: Advice from Those Who Have Been There. Ch. 2, Doing Well in College: Strategies for Success. Ch. 4, Understanding the Basics of Good Writing: How to Write in College and Other Formal Settings.

Classroom Activities: Introduction to course. Student Introduction to *Real Skills*. In-class diagnostic writing. In-class diagnostic grammar test. Learning-styles survey. Overview of the writing process.

Writing Assignment: Paragraph on steps students could take to stay in college.

Week Two

Reading Assignment: Ch. 5, Narrowing and Exploring Your Topic: How to Decide What to Write About. Narration and illustration coverage in Ch. 8, Developing Your Paragraph: Different Ways to Present Your Ideas. Ch. 10, The Complete Sentence: Key Parts to Know.

Classroom Activities: Practice choosing topics and prewriting. Review homework exercises.

Writing Assignment: Find and explore topics for narration and illustration paragraphs.

Week Three

Reading Assignment: Ch. 6, Writing Your Paragraph: How to Put Your Ideas Together. Ch. 11, Fragments: Sentences That Are Missing a Key Part.

Classroom Activities: Group work on effective topic sentences and specific details (see Practice Together activities in Chapter 6). Review homework exercises.

Writing Assignment: Write topic sentences for narration and illustration paragraphs. Find supporting details, examples, and facts.

Week Four

Reading Assignment: Comparison-and-contrast and argument coverage in Ch. 8, Developing Your Paragraph: Different Ways to Present Your Ideas. Ch. 12, Run-Ons: Two Sentences Joined Incorrectly.

Classroom Activities: Work on ordering details in narration and illustration paragraphs. Do group activities (Practice Together) in Chapters 8 and/or 12. Review homework exercises.

Writing Assignment: Finish arranging details for narration and illustration paragraphs. Begin prewriting and narrowing ideas for comparison-and-contrast and argument paragraphs.

Week Five

Reading Assignment: Ch. 13, Subject-Verb Agreement Problems: Subjects and Verbs That Do Not Match. Ch. 14, Verbs: The Past Tense.

Classroom Activities: Begin writing topic sentences for comparison-and-contrast and argument paragraphs and selecting supporting details. Do group activities (Practice Together) in Chapters 13 and/or 14. Review homework exercises.

Writing Assignment: Draft narration and illustration paragraphs.

Week Six

Reading Assignment: Ch. 7, Improving Your Paragraph: How to Make It the Best It Can Be. Ch. 15, Verbs: The Past Participle.

Classroom Activities: Arrange details for comparison-and-contrast and argument paragraphs. Introduce peer evaluation and have students review each other's narration and illustration drafts. Do group activities (Practice Together) in Chapters 7 and/or 15. Review homework exercises.

Writing Assignment: Revise narration and illustration paragraphs. Draft comparison-and-contrast and argument paragraphs.

Week Seven

Reading Assignment: Ch. 17, Pronouns: Using Substitutes for Nouns. Ch. 18, Adjectives and Adverbs: Describing *Which One?* or *How?* Ch. 19, Misplaced and Dangling Modifiers: Avoiding Confusing Descriptions.

Classroom Activities: Peer review of comparison-and-contrast and argument paragraphs. Do group activities (Practice Together) in Chapter 17, 18, or 19. Review homework exercises.

Writing Assignment: Revise comparison-and-contrast and argument paragraphs.

Week Eight

Reading Assignment: Ch. 9, Moving from Paragraphs to Essays: How to Write Longer Papers. Ch. 20, Illogical Shifts: Avoiding Inconsistencies. Ch. 22, Coordination: Joining Sentences with Related Ideas. Ch. 23, Subordination: Joining Sentences with Related Ideas.

Classroom Activities: Discuss the differences between paragraphs and essays. Assign or ask students to pick an essay topic. Do group activities (Practice Together) in Chapters 9 and/or 26. Review homework exercises.

Writing Assignment: Revise cause-and-effect and argument paragraphs.

Week Nine

Reading Assignment: Ch. 24, Parallelism: Balancing Ideas. Ch. 25, Word Choice: Using the Right Words. Appendix A, Succeeding on Tests.

Classroom Activities: Draft essays in class. Try to collect the essays at the end of the class. Answer questions about final exam. Review homework exercises.

Writing Assignment: None. Suggest that students use the time to study for the final exam and to time themselves on a sample writing for the writing exam. Consider giving them practice topics to work with.

Week Ten

Classroom Activities: Final preparation for, and completion of, final.

Writing Assignment: In-class writing final. Final grammar test.

Using the Ancillary Package

Real Skills is accompanied by a wealth of resources designed to make your life easier and to make students' time in the developmental writing course more productive. Here are a few comments and suggestions for how you can use these resources in your course.

Print Ancillaries

Instructor's Annotated Edition of Real Skills

The *Instructor's Annotated Edition* (IAE) is unique in that it was carefully designed as a teaching tool for instructors who all too often have less time than they would like for class preparation. It contains not only the answers to all exercises in the student text but also a series of teaching tips in the margins. In other words, as you page through a chapter, you will find suggestions for presenting material in class, discussion prompts, options for collaborative learning, ideas for teaching in the computer lab, ideas for teaching ESL students, advice for appealing to different learning styles, and cross-references to other parts of the book and other parts of the *Real Skills* package. All are presented right where you need them, on the pages of the book itself. These aids make the IAE a true teaching text, a convenient resource that organizes the materials and ideas you need to teach a good class. You might want to highlight the ones you plan to use. And if you have teaching tips for specific topics or chapters that you would like to see in the IAE for the next edition of *Real Skills,* I urge you to send them to us at *Real Skills,* Bedford/St. Martin's, 75 Arlington Street, Boston, MA 02116.

Practical Suggestions for Teaching Real Skills

In *Practical Suggestions* (the instructor's manual that you are reading right now), you will find sample class schedules; suggestions for assignments and class activities; and advice on grading, dealing with developmental writing students, planning your course, and working with computers. In other words, this volume contains everything you ever wanted to know about teaching developmental writing but were afraid to ask.

Whether you are an old pro or a newcomer in the field of developmental writing, you should find the sample schedules (presented earlier in this chapter)

beneficial in getting your course organized. Of course, what works for one instructor or one class may not work for another instructor or even for another class taught by the same instructor. However, the schedules and sample syllabus should give you a starting point for using *Real Skills* with your students.

If you are new to developmental writing, you should find the materials in *Practical Suggestions* especially helpful. I suggest that you pay particular attention to Chapter 2, Tips for New Instructors, which was written to give you a general feel for the developmental writing class. Not only does this chapter impart useful information, but it also provides emotional support.

Then, to get a clearer understanding of the type of students you will be teaching, read Chapter 3, Working with Developmental Writers. Although it is hard to pinpoint exactly what you will encounter in your particular classroom, this chapter will at least help prepare you by suggesting various approaches for dealing with different kinds of students and their needs.

As you progress into the semester and turn your attention to day-to-day concerns, you may want to consult the chapters on assessment, technology, critical thinking, and instructional approaches. Remember that the materials presented in this ancillary are just guidelines. As you become comfortable in the developmental writing classroom and familiar with *Real Skills,* you will probably adapt many of the suggestions and originate your own plans and assignments.

Additional Resources for Real Skills

Welcome *Additional Resources* with open arms, for it includes materials that will make your job as an instructor easier. Here you will find a diagnostic grammar pre-test and a post-test, additional exercises, and reproducible forms to aid your instruction. I always dreaded the arrival of a new text because I knew that I had to prepare new tests and perhaps new handouts and/or transparencies to match the terminology and content of the new book. Now, however, I can turn to *Additional Resources* for those materials and spend more time on actual class preparation, grading, and student conferences.

Teaching Developmental Writing: Background Readings

Do you ever want confirmation that what you are thinking and doing is right or at least on track with

other i   ctors? If so, then you will enjoy the selection   *Background Readings.* Chosen to help
both r   nd experienced teachers, these readings
cover   de variety of topics that concern the develop   al professional.

   F   if your approach to developmental writing,   ng, grammar instruction, or classroom ac-
tivit   as proved successful in the past, you may
be r   for something new. If that's the case, the
rea   offer advice and suggestions from experts
in t   eld and ordinary teachers in the trenches.
Ve   teachers—those who have been there and
no   y survived the experience but enjoyed it—
kn   est.

Reference Card

T   three-panel laminated card includes quick
v   g and editing advice and more. Have students
    it up next to their computer monitor for ref-
    ce as they write. This card can be packaged for
   with students' texts.

Bedford/St. Martin's ESL Workbook

   s handy workbook covers grammar issues for multi-
   gual students with varying English-language
   lls and cultural backgrounds. Instructional in-
   ductions are followed by illustrative examples
   d exercises. This supplement can be packaged for
   ee with students' texts.

   Note: If you teach in Florida, be aware that
From Practice to Mastery, a study guide for the
Florida College Basic Skills Exit Test, is also available with *Real Skills.* This guide can be packaged
for free with students' texts.

Electronic Ancillaries

Exercise Central
bedfordstmartins.com/realskills

One resource available through the Student Center
for *Real Skills* that will be especially useful to students
and instructors is *Exercise Central,* an online collection
of exercises related to writing, grammar, punctuation, sentence style, word choice, and ESL issues. This
collection is the largest available, with more than
9,000 items. It is thorough, simple to use, and convenient for you and your students. *Exercise Central*
includes multiple exercise sets at a variety of levels
as well as an interactive reporting feature. Students
receive customized, immediate feedback for all

their answers, usually including an explanation of
why the answers are correct or incorrect—feedback that turns practice into a learning experience.

When students enter *Exercise Central,* they will
gain access to a Customized Lesson Plan based on
the editing chapters in *Real Skills.* This lesson plan
will help students make the connection between
their online practice sessions and the content of the
book and the writing course. In addition, the Customized Lesson Plan will help students keep track
of which exercises they have completed and which
topics they need more practice with.

Each editing chapter in *Real Skills* appears in
the Customized Lesson Plan. Once students have
found the chapter they want to practice with, they
will immediately see a link to the primary exercises
for this topic (in the first column). These are exercises that have been written especially to accompany *Real Skills;* the level and coverage match those
in the text. You will probably want to direct most
students to start with the primary exercises. If students need additional practice, you might direct
them to another exercise at the same level; links to
other developmental exercises are included in the
lesson plan. If students have done well on the first
exercise, you might suggest that they practice further with another exercise at a higher level; links to
more difficult exercises are also included in the lesson plan.

To simplify the task of course management,
the reporting feature of *Exercise Central* allows you
to monitor the progress of individual students or
of the class as a whole; if you choose the latter option, you can see the results for a single exercise
set or for all exercise sets at once. If you have several classes or sections, you can even create customized reports that will display reports for each
class or section separately.

The first time you sign in to *Exercise Central*
as an instructor, you will be asked to register by
supplying some information about yourself, your
class, and your institution; you will also be asked
to give your e-mail address. Once the registration
process is complete, you will be sent a password by
e-mail. When you sign in using this password, you
will gain access to the instructor area of *Exercise
Central.* If you want to see reports on your students'
exercises, simply tell students to type in your e-mail
address when they sign in. You will be able to view
reports on all students who have supplied your
e-mail address. Complete directions for using the
reporting features of the new Gradebook are included in the Web site for *Exercise Central* itself.

WritingClass
www.yourwritingclass.com

WritingClass is an online course space shaped by the needs of developmental students. Loaded with instructional material, engaging activities, and simple writing tools, *WritingClass* presents assignments in a straightforward interface that helps students see what they have done and where they need to go next. This online course space helps students keep up with their assignments and lets them work whenever they have time, wherever they have Web access. In *WritingClass* you will find

- Diagnostics to help identify student problem areas.
- Personalized Study Plans for targeted practice.
- Developmental-level quizzes drawn from *Testing Tool Kit* question database.
- Hundreds of grammar exercises.
- *Make-a-Paragraph Kit* writing tutorials and exercises.
- A place for students to write and keep their drafts.

For more information on using *WritingClass*, visit www.yourwritingclass.com or see the Bedford/St. Martin's catalog page.

Student Center for Real Skills
bedfordstmartins.com/realskills

Send students to free and open resources, or upgrade to an expanding collection of innovative digital content—all in one place. The *Student Center for Real Skills* provides access to *Exercise Central*, the largest free online database of editing exercises (see above). Additional free resources include help with standardized tests, building vocabulary, and conducting a job search; annotated student paragraphs and essays; the VARK Learning Style Questionnaire; Grammar Girl podcasts; and useful forms mentioned in the book. Premium resources available through the *Student Center for Real Skills* include *WritingClass* and *Re: Writing Plus*.

Testing Tool Kit: A Writing and Grammar Test Bank CD-ROM

This CD-ROM, free to instructors using *Real Skills*, allows you to create secure, customized tests and quizzes from a pool of nearly 2,000 questions.

Ideal for assessing students' writing and grammar competency, the test bank can also be used to create practices that are tailored to course goals. Ten ready-to-administer diagnostic tests are also included. See the inside front cover of this manual for a chart that correlates topics in *Testing Tool Kit* with chapters in *Real Skills*.

Exercise Central to Go

This student CD-ROM provides hundreds grammar practice items. It can be packaged for with students' texts.

Make-a-Paragraph Kit CD-ROM

This fun, interactive CD-ROM inclu   an "Extreme Paragraph Makeover" animatic   eaching students about paragraph developme   s well as exercises that get students to buiid   ir own paragraphs. It also includes a set of   iovisual tutorials on the four most serious crr   and additional grammar practices. To ord   his CD-ROM, please contact your Bedford   Martin's sales representative or e-mail sal   support at **sales_support@bfwpub.com**.

Re: Writing
bedfordstmartins.com/r   riting

This Web site offers free access   even more writing and grammar exercises, mo   documents, useful Web links, advice on avoic   plagiarism, and more.

The I-Series of CD-ROM

Because there are some th   s you just cannot do in a book, Bedford/St. Ma   s now offers a unique line of CD-ROMs to teac   inciples of visual rhetoric (*ix*), argument (*i-cla*   and research and documentation (*i-cite*).

To see a demo of many of the electronic resources listed previously, or to place an order, visit **bedfordstmartins.com/thinking**.

2

Tips for New Instructors

Where Am I and How Did I Get Here?

Like instructors at many other colleges, you may have been assigned a developmental writing course without any or much advance warning. You should realize that you are in for a semester of interesting challenges. Developmental students offer the instructor an opportunity for a great sense of accomplishment. Of course, right now you may be asking yourself the much more fundamental question "How do I prepare for this class?"

First, remember that many of your students did not ask to be in a developmental course. Some have learning disabilities, emotional problems, physical disabilities, or disadvantaged backgrounds. Usually, their problems are not of their own making; they do not need to be penalized again. They are adults, so treat them as adults. Respect their individuality.

Second, commit yourself to your students. Being committed does not mean you must spend every waking moment with your students. In fact, you will probably need to set limits (allow yourself a lunch break, for instance) or your students may take over all of your office hours and more. Plus, if you are adjunct, your time on campus may be extremely tight and you may be commuting between campuses. However, remember that you are teaching students, not a subject. Commit yourself to helping them learn, and make your classes as interesting and as varied as possible. If you cannot cover as much content as you had planned, do not worry about it. You are the only one who will know. Your students will appreciate everything you do.

Third, have patience. If one student asks a question, two or three others will ask the same question. If you make an announcement in class,

three or more students will not hear it. If you ask for an assignment, several will claim that they did not know you wanted it. If possible, protect yourself by limiting the consecutive hours you will teach developmental classes; they are demanding because the students require so much personal attention. Fortunately, however, most of your students will want to please, and most will want to learn.

Fourth, be realistic in your expectations. Do not ask your students to do any work you have not tried beforehand. Work all the exercises yourself. That way, you not only discover which exercises to include and which to omit but also gain an idea of how long each assignment will take and how long you can maintain interest in it. If you get bored, your students certainly will. And if it takes you an hour to do the assignment, it will probably take them two to three hours, or more.

Fifth, find a supportive colleague. If you are teaching in a department where you are the only developmental instructor, find a colleague at a nearby college. Or find someone in your department who is sympathetic. You can always remind your colleagues that your developmental students will eventually move into their credit classes, so they need to take an interest in the developmental courses.

Sixth, find time for yourself and your professional growth. If at all possible, do not teach more than two-thirds of your load in developmental courses. Try to balance the levels of students you teach. (See Chapter 12, Surviving and Growing as a Professional, for more recommendations.)

Finally, take advantage of the instructional resources available and prepare thoroughly for class. *Real Skills* has a wealth of resources designed to make your life easier and your students' time in the developmental course more beneficial. (See

Chapter 1 of this manual for more on *Real Skills'* ancillary package.) Use them to plan your semester and each day. Students appreciate an instructor who is organized and on top of things.

Anticipating a Successful First Week

The keys to surviving the first week are preparation and flexibility. Prepare as thoroughly as you can what you want to happen on each day, even plotting out how many minutes you expect to spend on each activity. (Plan to do too much rather than too little—it is much more disturbing to run out of things to do before class is over than to have class end before you finish.) But remain flexible: No matter how carefully you plan, anything can happen.

Chapter 1 of this manual contains a section titled "What to Do on Day One." Read it and use it as a guide in your planning. Here is an overview of what you should hope to accomplish in the first week of class.

GIVE AN OVERVIEW OF THE COURSE. Distribute the syllabus and discuss the course focus.

ESTABLISH RAPPORT WITH AND AMONG STUDENTS. Give them a little pep talk about how much they can learn this semester. Try to establish a feeling of comfort and openness from the very start. Always ask for questions. Try an icebreaking activity. (See Creating a Comfortable Environment, right.)

ESTABLISH DEMEANOR. Let students know—either explicitly or through your own example—that you expect them to treat one another, themselves, and you with respect, and that you will do the same. Try to establish a sense of responsibility in the students and let them know that you are fair but serious about the class.

ESTABLISH ROUTINES AND POLICIES. Let students know the grading and attendance policies, tell them what textbooks and supplies they will need, and inform them of any daily routines (e.g., journal writing for the first ten minutes of class).

GET BASIC INFORMATION FROM STUDENTS. Have students fill out an information form that includes their e-mail addresses, phone numbers, class loads, and workloads. (See p. 3 for a sample form.)

ASSESS STUDENTS' NEEDS AND UNCOVER THEIR GOALS. Have students write a brief passage (150 words) so that you can assess their writing level and areas where improvement is needed. (See Chapter 1 of this manual for specific ideas about this first assignment.) Give them a diagnostic grammar test to evaluate their editing skills and needs. (*Additional Resources* includes a diagnostic test. The *Testing Tool Kit* CD-ROM with this book also includes diagnostics.)

HELP THEM GET ORGANIZED AND PREPARED FOR SUCCESS. Distribute an assignment schedule and show students how to use it; let them know that they will be responsible for making sure that their assignments are handed in on time and that they are well prepared for tests. Have students set up class notebooks using three-ring binders or another system. Let students know how important this tool is to their own success and how you expect them to maintain it. Many students do not know how to use a textbook, so walk them through the student introduction in *Real Skills,* which acquaints them with the features of the book.

Creating a Comfortable Environment

If you want students to learn, you need to make them feel comfortable in your classroom. Try to establish a sense of belonging. Make your classroom a place where students want to be and where they can feel free to participate. Let the students see that you want to be in that classroom with them and that you are there to help them.

Establishing a comfortable environment begins with the very first day. Many students appreciate a teacher who is not only friendly and open but also organized. Therefore, begin your first day with an overview of what you will study during the semester and how class will be conducted. Let them know when major assignments are due or when tests will be given. And, if you have an end-of-the-semester test that students have to take outside of class time, let them know when the tests are scheduled. When students know from the beginning what is expected of them and what to expect from you, they can relax and let the learning happen.

Beginning on the first day, you should also let students know that you are an understanding, although firm, teacher. Emphasize the importance of due dates and completed homework, but also convey that you know the unforeseen sometimes occurs. Encourage them to notify you in the event of an emergency so that you can work together to overcome any obstacles. Even if a particular student never experiences an emergency while in your class, he or she will appreciate your caring attitude and will be likely to open up about class problems.

Students need to feel comfortable not only with you but also with each other. Try some ice-breaking exercises at the beginning of the semester. For ideas, see page 5 of this manual. And if you ask students to share information about themselves, you should be willing to do the same. Both students and teachers need reminders that we are all human beings with feelings and lives outside the classroom. Students also enjoy hearing personal anecdotes. I do not mean sharing life stories, because you will discover that most students truly want to learn and do not want to waste time in class. However, if you can talk about writing or grammar problems that you, former students, friends, or family members have had, or use yourself as the subject of a writing project that you are doing with the students, the class will learn to see you as a person rather than as an authority figure to be feared.

A sense of humor is imperative. Do not take yourself too seriously. If you can laugh at yourself, your students can relax and will be less afraid to make mistakes. If your tongue gets tangled, make a funny face, babble for a couple of seconds, shake your head, laugh, and start over again. Reveal your own problems with grammar or spelling or writing. Illustrate how you handle your writing problems or how you learned a particularly difficult grammatical point.

Help students feel comfortable speaking up. Students should never feel as though the teacher thinks they are dumb. This is especially important when going over exercises in class; remember that not all exercises have a single right answer. Take time to think about the student's response, then say whether it is okay or whether another answer would be better. Do not hesitate to tell a student you need time to think about that answer because it is not the one you had thought of.

Becoming involved with the students and their work will help you create an atmosphere that is conducive to learning. Develop awareness of your students. Try to read their faces to determine when someone is having problems. Do not hesitate to offer assistance if you think a student needs help. Students believe that teachers who provide individual attention are demonstrating that they want the student to learn the material, not just get a grade.

Believe it or not, a comfortable environment in the classroom can also depend on your accessibility outside the classroom. Have flexible office hours and an open-door policy. Remember that you have probably set up your office hours to accommodate your own schedule, but your students have work, home, and class schedules that may not coincide with yours. Also, like you, they may have problems, such as sick children or court dates, that may occur during your class time or office hours. Therefore, be willing to meet students early in the morning or to stay late in the afternoon if a student has to make up a test or needs assistance with a writing assignment. Or work out mutually convenient alternatives such as a prearranged phone conference. This alternative works well, especially for adjunct faculty. You might also encourage students to find a buddy to share phone numbers with; then, if they are absent or do not understand an assignment, they will have someone to call if you cannot be reached.

Encouraging Class Participation

Someone could earn a million dollars by coming up with a formula for making students participate in all classes. Unfortunately, what works in some classes won't work in others. Remember that your attitude does more to encourage or discourage class participation than you might think. Whether you are grading, lecturing, or going over homework, remain positive. Many of your developmental students will have low self-esteem and need positive reinforcement, so provide lots of verbal praise and encouragement. Here are some other ideas.

Give Credit for Participation

Even if your college uses the pass/fail system for developmental courses, most of your students will want to earn good grades and will strive for an A. So give credit for work other than tests or papers whenever you can.

Give homework checks. When students complete an assignment—answering questions, preparing an outline, writing a rough draft, or completing grammar exercises—put a check in your grade book. The checks can be tabulated as points for a certain percentage of the student's final average. One way to encourage attendance is to have a firm policy not to accept late homework; therefore, the grade could encourage students to attend class prepared. (You will probably want to make such a statement in your syllabus and/or on your daily schedule.) The more often students come to class with completed homework, the higher their homework grade. When they realize they will get credit only when they attend class with their homework ready, many will make a greater effort to get to school. But also encourage students to show up whether or not their homework is complete. Tell them that they can still benefit from being in class.

Plan In-Class Activities

Go over assignments in class. If the assignment will lead to a test, comment on how the exercises or rules will apply to the test, or point out which exercises resemble items that will be on the test. If students realize that they will get help toward a test or help with their problems during class, they may be more likely to attend and participate.

Also, while going over assignments, ask students to provide answers (allowing them plenty of time, if needed). (For more on the need for "wait time," see p. 56.) You can go around the room and have each student answer a question. You can also call on individual students. Do not always rely on volunteers; often, the same students will be the first to respond. When the class expects a particular student to have the right answer to every question, others will stop trying.

Plan in-class work days that allow students to get one-on-one assistance from you without a grade. When individuals know that you are willing to help them find the solution to a grammar exercise or to a problem sentence, they will be more willing to speak up during whole-class discussions.

Although some students complain about small-group work, many believe that it offers them a chance to learn a lot and to establish a bond with other classmates. Some students enjoy small-group work because they find it less threatening or intimidating than participating in whole-class discus-

sions. Others may enjoy being chosen as the spokesperson who will give an oral summary or report of the group's activity.

Managing the Classroom

Encouraging student participation and varying the class activities are probably the two most helpful classroom management techniques. When students are actively engaged in learning, both they and you will be happier and more productive. The following are some recommendations for channeling the energy of your students and handling occasional disruptions.

LET STUDENTS KNOW THE COURSE REQUIREMENTS AND YOUR EXPECTATIONS. Make it clear that students are responsible for meeting them both. Students should know that you expect them to be on time and to remain until dismissed. In signing up for a course, they have agreed to meet at the specified hours; if they do not hold up their end of this agreement, they should be counted tardy or absent. Let students know that you will penalize late papers and missed tests. Also establish a deadline for accepting late work or makeup work (for example, one week past the original due date). Clearly outlining your expectations in the syllabus will help prevent students from misunderstanding what you require from them.

You may want to prepare a "student responsibilities" page so that students can read and keep an outline of their commitments; they should return a signed note to you agreeing to those terms. On page 27 is a sample Acknowledgment of Student Responsibilities. You can adapt the statement to fit your own course requirements.

Survey of Interests

Please take a few minutes to complete this brief survey. The information you provide will help me to create assignments that draw on your experiences and interests, so that the writing you do in this course is connected to your life and your goals.

1. When you are not doing schoolwork, what kinds of magazines and books do you read?

2. What are two of your favorite hobbies and/or extracurricular activities? (Please be relatively serious here.)

3. What commitments and responsibilities do you have outside of school? (for example: work, child care, or other family responsibilities; membership in a group or organization)

4. What is your own assessment of your writing abilities, and what in particular would you like to learn from this writing class?

5. Turn this page over, and on the back side, write a one-paragraph letter to a friend, explaining to him or her how you *feel* about taking this writing course.

Thank you for taking the time to complete this survey.

Acknowledgment of Student Responsibilities

As a student in Developmental Writing, I know that I need to take the responsibility for my own success. Therefore, I will

- attend class regularly,
- do assigned work,
- ask for assistance when I need it,
- participate in class activities,
- notify my instructor of any emergencies or problems.

Please sign the statement at the bottom, tear it off, and return it to your instructor.

I have read the Acknowledgment of Student Responsibilities and understand my options and responsibilities.

Signed: _____

Date: _____

Class Time: _____

REWARD TIME SPENT ON TASK. Homework and in-class activities are important factors in learning. If you ask students to do an assignment, show them that it is important by taking class time to discuss the correct responses and to answer questions they may have. Depending on the exercise, you can have students give an oral group response, go around the room and have each student answer one question, or divide the class into small groups to work with assignments. However, do not feel obligated to grade each piece of work. You can give homework checks for completed, ungraded work and in-class activities.

BE PREPARED TO DEAL WITH PLAGIARISM. Your colleagues have occasionally encountered student papers that borrow either language or ideas or both, and so will you. If you suspect plagiarism, try to pinpoint specific words or sections that you are concerned about. Then, decide if the plagiarism is the result of inadequate documentation or of an outright attempt to submit the writing of someone else. If you think that a student has copied from another source, you might ask a colleague or a librarian if the piece sounds familiar. You might also enter key phrases from the paper into a search engine to see if you turn up any sources that use identical language. Do not confront a student unless you are prepared to back up your accusation. Even when I have found the original piece, I have given the student the opportunity to confess by asking how he or she arrived at the final version or where he or she got the information. By requiring in-class writing and keeping some of a student's original work in a file, you can guard against plagiarism. In addition, by requiring that all drafts and research notes (if appropriate) be included with the final copy, you can see how the student's writing has evolved from the initial draft. However, if you worry about the possibility of plagiarism, you can develop and distribute a policy similar to the one on page 29.

Also, consider referring to the Bedford/St. Martin's Workshop on Plagiarism, at **bedfordstmartins .com/plagiarism**, which offers advice on avoiding and detecting plagiarism, with downloadable handouts for students.

Plagiarism Policy

The *Random House Dictionary* defines plagiarism as follows: "The appropriation or imitation of the language, ideas, and thoughts of another author, and representation of them as one's original work." The most obvious form of plagiarism is copying directly from printed or Web-based materials without using quotation marks. A less obvious form, but equally as serious, is summarizing or paraphrasing the *ideas* of an author without citing the author as a source. Additionally, a third type of plagiarism that students must be aware of is using an editor—whether a friend, family member, or tutor—beyond a reasonable level. In this instance, the student's paper does not reflect the knowledge, voice, and/or style of the student author.

Improper or inadequate documentation will often lower a paper's score. In the case of plagiarism, however, no credit is given for a paper. In order to protect both students and faculty members, the following procedures may be followed when an instructor suspects plagiarism:

1. The instructor will indicate to the student that the paper is plagiarized and gets no credit.

2. The student may appeal the instructor's decision to the English Department Chair.

3. The department will have the student write a similar paper under supervision. (In cases of works of literature, the topic assigned will be from the same work that the student explored in the first paper.)

4. The department's designated readers will determine if the second paper parallels the first in sophistication of ideas, knowledge, syntax, punctuation, voice, diction, and style.

5. If designated readers agree that the paper does not reflect the work of the student, the first paper will not be accepted. On the other hand, if the designated readers agree that the two papers are written by the same person, the instructor will award credit for the first paper.

Sample Writing Assignments

Real Skills is filled with writing assignments for paragraphs. However, every instructor appreciates having a handy compendium of all-purpose writing prompts, useful for filling a sudden gap in the class schedule. The following are a few that have worked for me. (For journal writing prompts, please see the section on journals in Chapter 8.)

Essay Topics

NARRATION:

> Tell a brief story that is well known in your family.

ILLUSTRATION:

> Ways a college education will improve my life
>
> Three changes I would make if I could start my life over
>
> The worst job I ever had
>
> My proudest accomplishment

DESCRIPTION:

> The most relaxing place I have ever been
>
> My favorite holiday

PROCESS ANALYSIS:

> How to make a good impression on a first date
>
> How to give up a bad habit

CLASSIFICATION:

> Types of students
>
> Types of music or movies
>
> Ways of handling a problem

DEFINITION:

> A good or bad student, teacher, parent, or friend
>
> Happiness
>
> Success

COMPARISON/CONTRAST:

> Two ways parents can handle their teenagers' problems
>
> Two different jobs I have held or hope to hold
>
> The different styles or techniques of two athletes or teachers

CAUSE/EFFECT:

> The effect of pressure on students to get good grades
>
> The effects of viewing pornography

ARGUMENT:

> Colleges should (should not) require admission tests.
>
> Colleges should (should not) provide a day-care center.
>
> High schools should (should not) teach sex education.
>
> The government should (should not) provide free higher education for everyone.

Words of Advice

Everyone you talk to will have a different piece of advice on how to handle a class. My advice on how to survive emotionally is that when you first walk into a developmental classroom, you should realize that you do not have and will not have complete control over your students. You must understand that many factors influence your students, and their outside activities and obligations take them away from class and study time. An important task is to teach a student that he or she is someone you care about helping. When you do that, you are well on your way to success in the developmental classroom. Even if you think you are not making a difference, one student can let you know you have succeeded. Sometimes, one student is all it takes.

What follows are some words of advice from experienced instructors across the country. If you have your own words of advice that you would like us to include in the next edition of *Practical Suggestions*, please send them to us at *Real Skills*, Bedford/St. Martin's, 75 Arlington Street, Boston, MA 02116.

> Students neither live nor learn in a vacuum; we must help them integrate what they learn in the academy and what they bring from their lives. They then complete the cycle of real learning by letting their academic discoveries inform their life choices. We can give them voices in the classroom by evoking what they bring with them; we give them voices in the real world as we nurture essential critical reading, writ-

ing, and thinking skills. We want those at risk to become active, successful students as we help them develop the skills needed to be active, successful citizens. Many at-risk students give themselves only one chance to succeed in the academy; it is up to us to make that chance count!

—Sandra M. Carey
Lexington Community College, Kentucky

Be open to the lessons hidden in all that comes your way.
—James F. Rice
Quinsigamond Community College, Massachusetts

I suggest that teachers who are new to developmental writing and to developmental students should read Mina Shaughnessy's *Errors and Expectations* for some sound thinking about developmental writing, Mike Rose's *Lives on the Boundary* for insight into developmental writers and readers, and Frank Smith's writings on the writing–reading connection. Smith's ideas about the "literary club" are very important. These three books give a lot of background and argue for hope and enthusiasm in teaching developmental writers. Good luck!

—Jack O'Keefe
Daley College, Illinois

First, make sure you understand why you want students to do a particular assignment, then make sure you articulate the "why" to your students. If you are fuzzy, then your students will produce fuzzy responses. Also, make sure you have figured out how the assignment could be done   if you have done the proper "fiddling" with the "ins" and "outs" and "ways" and "means," you can provide a clearer road map for your students. This is crucial.

—Beverly Ann Butler
Shippensburg University, Pennsylvania

Really know what the developmental writing course objectives and outcomes are. Also, know the writing expectations in the next-level writing courses and in content area courses.

Do intensive diagnostic work with your students. Investigate their attitude toward writing, their interests, their goals as well as their mechanical problems. Address more than just the misplaced comma; deal with the whole student.

Enjoy! Create a classroom environment that stimulates real discussion about topics and writing. Be creative; be excited about what you are teaching and what you are writing. Write with your students.

—Patricia A. Malinowski
Finger Lakes Community College, New York

"Passive" student behavior often in   tes resistance to the syllabus rather than indifference. Read Shor's "The First Day of Class" in *Backgroun ings* (excerpted from *Empowering Educatio* gestions about working with resistan read and discuss Shor's essay with   nts. Solicit student ideas for improvin   se. I've made important changes to the   abus based on student suggestions. Students have provided feedback during class discussions, as part of written assignments, in e-mail postings, and in anonymous letters written in class. I welcome this exchange as an opportunity to research student concerns—and my own teaching practices.

—Susan Naomi Bernstein
University of Cincinnati

Be wary of all the new technology that purports to offer solutions that will solve education's perceived woes. Teaching is still a human covenant between student and teacher. A reassuring smile or an encouraging pat on the back will often accomplish more than any of the "bells and whistles."

—Steve Whiting
Sinclair Community College, Ohio

Creating a climate of trust, respect, and awareness of differences and cultures is crucial for students' (and an instructor's) success in the developmental writing classroom. From day one, you, as leader, need to be proactive in setting the tone. Figure out where students are in the writing process . . . what they already know . . . what they feel confident about, and build from that point. Praise the positives, and give them tools to "fix" what they need to work on to reach competency in standard academic English writing.

Vary assignments and readings, if you use them, to appeal to different ages and cultural or language backgrounds. Especially for second-language students or internationals, be aware of cultural differences in writing styles and openly acknowledge them. "Your way of writing has worked for you in the past, but your professors will expect _____. Here's how to produce _____." Approach grammar, spelling, and punctuation as part of an editing and proofreading task that you always do before completing a manuscript. Don't make them a first-draft nightmare.

Avoid putting people on the spot. At the same time, give shy students a turn at being leader in a small group, or ask them to be "secretary" at the board, taking board notes on class discussion. Share leadership. One strategy that works well is to randomly pick a student and ask him or her to demonstrate at the board (for the benefit of absentees) a point you covered in the previous class. As the student "teaches" the class, take a chair and listen attentively. Have students in small groups photocopy their notes and share with others.

Use (and believe in) the idea that we're all here to learn more about writing—you, too. Take advantage of resources: listservs, online writing labs, e-mail. Some of your students may already have set up home pages on the Web; perhaps they can teach you about cyberspace writing or communicate with each other.

—Jan Bone
Roosevelt University, Illinois

Don't be intimidated by quiet classes. Enable students to explore their own personal experiences through their writing, knowing that every writer has at least one story that he or she can relate better than anyone else, and you may be the only person who may be given the privilege to read it.

—H. L. Phillips
Collin County Community College, Texas

Although collaborative work in the writing classroom is very popular and often quite successful, teachers should be careful in assessing group projects. Particularly, teachers should never give "group grades" for group writing projects. Teachers can reward collaboration and individual effort by having each group member assign the other group members a grade based upon a set of criteria established before the project begins. Students should write their rationale for the grades they assign to their fellow students and should submit their grade suggestions in sealed envelopes. This method produces more accountable students and less resentment toward students who fail to do their part in the collaborative process.

—Lisa Windham
College of the Mainland, Texas

Developmental writers need to understand that they have all the words they need to express themselves well. What we as teachers can give them is the confidence to express these words honestly, as close to their thinking as possible. And confidence comes with something to say, knowing what it is that we think or believe and why. Many students have definite opinions; not all of them realize the power that comes with evidence, the evidence of personal or researched reading material. So my advice to new instructors of writing is to enliven your writing classes with reading materials you love or respect, engage students in lively discussions of them, discussions that encourage the students to relate their own experiences, and then make them write and write and write some more.

—Francine L. DeFrance
Cerritos College, California

Sometimes, we just have to shut up. Not an easy thing to do. Especially for English teachers. And yet silence can be a highly effective tool, especially in writing conferences. As we sit with students, going over their writing, we often ask students questions, hoping that they'll see the sentence problem or the need for a transition or a supporting detail. We ask leading questions, questions like, "Hmm, something seems to be missing here. What do you think is missing?" And the student, knowing full well from past experience that questions asked by teachers are often rhetorical questions, waits for the teacher to answer. Which we usually do if a response isn't immediately forthcoming. Because we feel uncomfortable with the silence that hangs there. And because there are usually more students queued up waiting their turn. It's not easy playing the waiting game. But it is essential, for the student eventually becomes uncomfortable with silence, and then the student begins to think about the situation, to look at the writing, to venture a response. The student thus becomes a participant in a discussion, not simply a listener. The trick is to let the student know that you do expect a response and that if it takes a little time to think things through, well, that's okay. Our primary goal as writing teachers is to help students see for themselves—not to correct their writing or edit their papers. In order to help them see, sometimes we just have to be quiet.

—Tim McLaughlin
Bunker Hill Community College, Massachusetts

When I teach developmental writing classes, I see myself as a role model for students learning to be college students and participants in an academic community. As such, I try to teach them how to be college students: how to speak and write, yes, but also how to apply for financial aid, how to avoid test anxiety, how to work with other students, how to use a word processor, and so on. I believe that anything I can do to elevate their self-esteem by making them feel a part of the college is immensely valuable to their success.

—Elizabeth Boote Griffey
Florida Community College
at Jacksonville, Florida

One of the challenges of teaching an introductory writing course is that it is usually a requirement—students have to take it and instructors have to teach it. I try to subvert the "have to" atmosphere of the course right away by telling students how excited I am to teach the course. Before they even look at a syllabus, I let them know that this is an important thing for me to do, that I enjoy immensely the task of working with beginning writers, and that writing is something that I love and want other people to love. I find this approach is effective in clearing out any preconceptions about the drudgery of the course.

—Anne Aronson
Metropolitan State University, Minnesota

3

Working with Developmental Writers

The Typical Student

What kind of students will you face when you walk into a developmental classroom? To borrow from an old saying, every kind under the sun. That is what makes teaching a developmental writing class so exciting. Every student is unique, yet many share similar experiences, frustrations, and problems. Perhaps the best introduction to a typical student is through the words of some students themselves. Read how April, a twenty-year-old high school graduate, describes her experiences:

> My first semester in college has been wonderful. I started out scared, but suddenly things changed for the better. I had never attended college, so when I was told that I had to take a placement test, I really became annoyed and terrified more than ever. I've never done very well on tests. And when I failed that test, I was ashamed to call home and tell my parents that I was taking resource classes for the dumb. But after attending and participating in the classes, I discovered that the class was not for dumb people but for the ones who lacked knowledge in certain areas. I had never liked English, but as I started to pay more attention to the teacher and what she was saying, my feelings for English started to change. I can truly say that my teacher taught me something that I will carry on with me throughout life: I can do anything if I just work at it. I appreciate my teacher for showing and teaching me that I can do the work without feeling like I am in a remedial class.

Consider also the experiences of an older student who had feelings similar to April's. At age thirty-five, Anthony found himself in a developmental English class, but that did not seem to bother him. After two weeks of school, he wrote the following journal entry.

> School is fun. I haven't been in a classroom in seventeen years, so I'm excited about being a student. I am enrolled in twelve hours, which makes me a full time student. My first day was a disaster because I slept through most of my English class. I hated myself for doing that, and the next day I apologized and explained to my teacher that I hadn't been in school for seventeen years. She told me not to worry because she would make sure she'd bring me up to college level. To some, maybe that means nothing, but to me that took a load off. For, you see, that was my first class, and her encouragement made me feel I could make it.

You probably became a teacher because you wanted to reach students, to change a life or two. Developmental writing classes give you that opportunity every semester. In order to help your students, you need to understand them. These students may not be the same kinds of students that you have previously taught. Teaching a developmental course may be challenging and frustrating, yet it can also be rewarding because of the mixed population. For instance, in a class of twenty-five students, five may have goofed off and not taken the placement test seriously; three may be nonnative speakers; three may have enrolled to increase self-confidence; three to five may have serious learning disabilities and have little chance of completing the course in one semester (or two); three may be repeating the course; and the remainder may recognize that their skills are lacking and that they need the remedial instruction that the course offers. Some students start asking questions the minute they walk in the door, interrupt class to ask the same questions repeatedly, and remain after class to ask more questions. Other students resent being in a developmental class and may offer great resistance and a surly attitude. Some may be recent high school graduates, whereas others may have dropped out of high school or college years before and are trying again. With so many personal and academic needs, it is a constant struggle to keep all students interested and progressing.

In addition to recognizing the variety of reasons students have for enrolling in your class, you need to understand their academic styles and attitudes toward learning. Many may have one or more of the following characteristics:

- Genuine desire to understand

- Hope for a better life through education

- Enthusiastic approach to learning

- Low self-esteem or lack of self-confidence

- Little motivation

- Procrastination

- Few organizational skills

- Avoidance of challenges

- Erratic attendance

- Tendency to make excuses for poor performances

- Little practice with reading and therefore with using written models for writing

- Interference from another language (if the student comes from a non–English-speaking country)

Although the variety may seem impossible to deal with in one class, you can find some common ground. In certain ways, developmental writers share common needs. No matter what category a given student falls into, these developmental writers need

- Instruction in basic grammar, punctuation, and syntax.

- Help in thinking.

- Help in organizing thoughts.

- Patterns, formulas, or models to follow when they start to write.

- Assistance in learning how to study and to complete assignments.

- Lots of encouragement and positive reinforcement.

- Assistance in learning how to read critically, assimilate information, and respond to ideas.

- Revision techniques that work.

You probably will find it easy to teach motivated, focused students. Perhaps the biggest and most rewarding challenges of teaching developmental writers, however, come from those students who have experienced years of failure and frustration owing to conditions beyond their control. Many of your students have a history of learning disabilities, school transfers, family obligations, or personal problems that caused them to drop out or underachieve. Yet each is an individual who deserves the best education you can offer. As a teacher of developmental writers, you need to recognize the various backgrounds and remain sensitive to the individual needs of all students.

Students with Special Needs

Although most of *Practical Suggestions* discusses developmental students in general terms, you may benefit from a more in-depth look at certain special needs students. Suggestions for teaching ESL students are found in Chapter 9.

Learning-Disabled Students

A learning disability is a permanent disorder that affects the way people take in, retain, and express information. The incoming or outgoing information may become scrambled between the eye or ear and the brain. Learning-disabled (LD) adults often have deficits in one or more of the following areas: reading comprehension, spelling, written expression, math comprehension, and problem solving. Occasionally, they also experience problems with organizational skills, time management, and social skills. Many LD adults may have language-based and/or perception problems. Some studies report that two out of every ten people have some form of learning dysfunction; other studies indicate that four or more out of every ten people may have a learning disability.[1]

In LD students' writing, you will probably notice problems with sentence structure (fragments, run-ons and comma splices, poor grammar) and

[1] *Sources:* Harold N. Levinson, *Smart but Feeling Dumb* (New York: Warner, 1984), and Jovita M. Ross-Gordon, "Adults with Learning Disabilities: An Overview for the Adult Educator," Information Series, no. 337 (Columbus: ERIC Clearinghouse on Adult, Career, and Vocational Education, Center on Education and Training for Employment, The Ohio State University, 1989) [ERIC no. ED 315 664].

spelling (omissions, substitutions, transpositions). LD students may write slowly, have poor penmanship, or copy incorrectly from a book or a blackboard. Orally, they may have difficulty expressing ideas (even those they seem to understand), speak incorrect English, or have trouble concentrating on and comprehending spoken language. They may have difficulty following oral and written directions, demonstrate a short attention span during lectures, be slow to start and complete tasks, and need help in time management.

When teaching writing, emphasize and practice the connection between listening, speaking, reading, and writing. Use the suggestions for discussion printed in the margins of the *Instructor's Annotated Edition of Real Skills*, encourage class discussion, and have students talk in complete, grammatically correct sentences. Teaching writing as a process helps the LD students monitor their progress through an assignment and keeps the assignment from becoming overwhelming. Break the written assignments into stages, assessing and responding to each stage (e.g., prewriting, outlining, drafting, peer editing, revising). Encourage students to use the steps and outlines in Chapter 8 of *Real Skills*; these make the paragraph-writing process manageable. Although you may think that a formal structure is too limiting for writers, LD students find that, rather than constraining them, structure or format helps them generate a paper. Try having them use the planning forms provided in *Additional Resources*. Once they learn the form, they will become more comfortable with writing and can branch out beyond that model.

In addition, you can help LD students—and all students, for that matter—by using the following suggestions:

- Provide a detailed course syllabus that outlines expectations, grading, material to be covered, due dates, and major tests.

- Start each class with an outline of what you plan to cover, and end each class with a summary of key points.

- Give assignments both orally and in writing to avoid confusion.

- Allow students to record lectures.

- Announce reading assignments well in advance so that students who are using recorded texts will have time to obtain the recordings.

- Provide study questions for exams that demonstrate the exam's format as well as its content.

- If necessary, allow LD students to demonstrate mastery of course material by means of alternative methods (e.g., extended time limits for testing, individually proctored exams in a separate room).

- Provide adequate opportunities for questions and answers.

- Write important information on the blackboard, use transparencies or PowerPoint slides, or prepare handouts to help students identify and remember key points. (See *Additional Resources* for transparency and handout masters.)

- Teach study skills and foster organization by requiring a class notebook.

- Use a variety of approaches to appeal to various learning styles.

- Be patient.

By law, schools must provide auxiliary aids for students who identify themselves as having learning disabilities, as well as for students with physical handicaps. It is the student's responsibility to notify the college about his or her specific situation and the appropriate or required aids. The school must provide such services as recorded texts, note takers, interpreters, readers, or student tutors. As the teacher, you might need to allow an extended time for reading assignments, testing in another location, recordings of lectures, printed notes so students can read along as you talk, or other such accommodations. If your college has a special department that deals with special needs or learning challenged students, contact it for assistance. That department will likely provide the services your students need and help you with testing. However, the greatest success will come when you and the student sit down together to determine what will work best for that student in your course. The results can be rewarding for both you and your student.

Dyslexic Students

Some studies estimate that as many as one in every seven students suffers from dyslexia to some degree, with approximately ten million Americans affected. Primarily, dyslexia is the inability to break down a word into its parts, with the reader/listener having difficulty distinguishing the individual sounds that letters and/or combinations of letters represent.

Historically, educational systems have relied on reading and writing to convey information and to test achievement; as a result, dyslexics are often viewed as having low intelligence. However, dyslexics often perceive more and formulate mental concepts more rapidly than other people. In fact, dyslexics often excel on the job, even if they are functionally illiterate. They may be visual, multidimensional thinkers who are intuitive and highly creative and who often excel at hands-on learning. They merely have difficulty processing letters, symbols, and words. In addition, students with dyslexia may have short-term memory difficulties; therefore, new information needs to be given more than once and those students need to concentrate much more than other students.

Develop a holistic approach when teaching dyslexics. First, present an overview of the unit or explain why you are doing a particular activity. Once they know the whole picture, they generally will approach the parts willingly. The Understand section at the beginning of most chapters in *Real Skills* may be especially useful to these students. When you break down processes into steps, allow time for feedback to check understanding. Avoid reinforcing failure by using dictation exercises or forcing students to copy words they cannot see correctly. Encourage the use of technology, such as spelling dictionaries, computers, and grammar checkers. Remind your students of spelling strategies or memory aids. Many dyslexics learn by talking, so set up group activities in which students can explain concepts to each other; use the suggestions for discussion, learning style, and teamwork printed in the margins of the *Instructor's Annotated Edition of Real Skills*.

When making writing assignments, be specific and write everything down; do not expect students to remember your oral instructions. Also, provide samples of the assignment and offer help with planning, structure, and organization. Focus on following set patterns (e.g., introduction, body, conclusion), identifying main points, distinguishing relevant from irrelevant details, and ordering points. In other words, give your students as many structural aids and formulas as you can.

Remember that dyslexics may be easily distracted by noise, activity, or visual "clutter." They may need more time than other students do to absorb information and to work through the outside distractions. If you use a blackboard during your discussion, erase the board before presenting a new idea so that students can concentrate on one point at a time. In addition, try to break up learning sessions and discussions to give students enough time to process the information.

Usually, by the time the dyslexic student appears in your college class, his or her self-esteem has become greatly eroded. Restoring a student's self-esteem will probably be the best and most important technique you can use to help your dyslexic students (or students with any learning problems) succeed.

Students with Attention-Deficit/ Hyperactivity Disorder

Although many people think of small children when they hear the term *attention-deficit/hyperactivity disorder* (ADHD), teenagers and adults can also suffer from this syndrome. In fact, some of your troublemakers might suffer from ADHD and not know it. Do not think that ADHD indicates a lack of intelligence. Quite the contrary—ADHD students often show signs of creativity and high intelligence. The following characteristics can help you identify an ADHD student:

- **A sense of underachievement.** Many ADHD students believe they are failures because they have trouble reaching their goals. This lack of self-esteem often results from years of being told they are lazy or different, or from frustrations caused by lack of success in projects.

- **Restlessness.** Although teenagers and adults do not always have the pronounced inability to stay still that we see in ADHD children, they can display fidgetiness through drumming fingers, swinging legs, shifting positions, or repeatedly getting up from the desk.

- **Difficulty getting organized.** ADHD students are easily overwhelmed by the tasks of daily living and are chronically late or chronically in a hurry. They can succeed if someone helps them get organized.

- **Chronic procrastination or trouble getting started.** Because they fear doing something incorrectly, ADHD students may become anxious and put off tasks numerous times. Similarly, some ADHD students exhibit enthusiastic beginnings but cannot follow through and thus have poor endings. Either of these traits leads to inconsistent work performance.

- **Impulsive behavior.** ADHD students have a tendency to say what comes to mind without necessarily considering the timing or appropriateness of the remark. Tied closely to impulsiveness is impatience, with a low tolerance for frustration. This frustration with not being able to do things the "right" way can manifest itself in an inability to follow proper procedure or go through established channels.

- **A tendency to become easily bored or distracted.** Because they have trouble focusing attention, ADHD students have a tendency to mentally drift away or tune out. The ADHD student exhibits poor listening skills and, when reading, may skip around or go to the end first.

- **A tendency to worry.** ADHD students seem to worry endlessly and experience a sense of impending doom, partly as a result of frustrations and previous failures.

If you know or suspect a student has ADHD, you can do the following: in one-on-one talk, make sure the student has comprehended the assignment; allow for reasonable freedom of movement within the classroom; vary the activities for the day; and constantly offer feedback and encouragement.

Adult Learners

Unlike some of their younger counterparts, adult students have often gone to great effort to enroll in college courses and are highly motivated to learn. They generally view learning as a means to an end, not an end in itself, though they may also want to do well in college to increase or maintain a sense of self-esteem.

When designing the curriculum, keep in mind that adults are usually goal oriented. They desire a course that is organized into clearly defined elements, and they prefer content presented in a straightforward, "how-to" approach. Also, adults have a wealth of life experiences and want to integrate new ideas with what they already know; in fact, such integration helps them retain and use the new information. Integrating the real world into the classroom comes naturally to these students and is one of the strategies most likely to ensure their success. (See Chapter 4, Bringing the Real World into the Classroom.) Most adults prefer self-directed learning over group learning experiences because self-direction gives them control over the pace. However, self-direction does not mean total isolation. Adult learners want other people as resources or guides. Therefore, one-on-one sessions work well with these students. You can serve as a facilitator while encouraging them to assume responsibility for their learning.

Within the classroom, remember that adult learners' self-esteem is constantly on the line. They tend to take errors personally, so stress that they will learn from their mistakes. To help them build self-confidence in the learning experience, clarify all expectations before getting into the actual lesson. Let these students know where you are heading with the assignments and how the class will help them reach their own goals. Adult students usually prefer to participate actively in the learning process. Many adult learners will tell you that they are irritated by long lectures that leave no time for practice. In sum, remember that adults want learning to be problem oriented, personalized, and self-directed.

Some of the best ways to motivate adult learners are to align the course content with their reasons for enrolling, decrease any barriers, and create a comfortable learning environment. Should problems arise, you need to discover what is keeping your students from learning. Because people learn at different speeds, it is natural for them to be anxious or nervous when faced with a timed learning situation. Positive reinforcement can enhance learning, as can specific feedback.

Creating a Productive Environment and Motivating Students

Whether your students are traditional freshmen, nonnative speakers, individuals with learning disabilities, or adult learners, they can all benefit from a classroom environment that encourages productivity and motivation. The following strategies will help foster students' ability—and their willingness—to learn.

SIMPLIFY OBJECTIVES AND LEARNING. Make sure instructions are clear and written down for students to check. Be clear in your own communications by making handouts easily comprehensible. Be explicit in your expectations. You may want to write main points and goals for the day on the board. You could divide the board into two sections. On the left, write what you hope to accomplish that day; on the right, remind students of the next assignment. That way, students know when they arrive in class what to expect and what you expect of them.

Also, remember to include oral assistance as well as written assistance. You can record important class lectures or respond orally to certain texts. In addition, some computer programs have sound, allowing students to hear instructions and even lessons.

HELP STUDENTS FEEL COMFORTABLE WITH THE PHYSICAL ACT OF WRITING. Students who have difficulty writing may feel more confident using an erasable pencil than permanent ink. One instructor has had great success with the erasable pen because it helps her introduce the importance of a professional-looking product while giving her students the ability to erase. Given that many developmental students have poor handwriting skills, you might want to ask your class to skip every other line as they write—this can improve readability not only for you but also for the students themselves as they edit and revise. Using computers can also relieve stress, so you may want to encourage students to type their assignments. Not only does learning to operate a computer offer a lifelong skill, but word processors enable many students to see more clearly what they have written, eliminate the drudgery of handwriting, help with organization, and aid in spelling and punctuation.

REINFORCE GOOD STUDY SKILLS. Help your students learn to budget time by giving them an estimate on how long a particular assignment will take or giving them clues about how much time to spend on each stage of longer assignments. Give them a daily schedule that details reading assignments, homework, tests, and due dates for writing assignments. Encourage your students to prioritize their responsibilities, and work with them to establish goals. Assigning Chapter 2 of *Real Skills*, Doing Well in College: Strategies for Success, is a good first step.

MAINTAIN A SUPPORTIVE ENVIRONMENT. Help students feel satisfaction when they are successful. Sometimes just a few encouraging words or actions are sufficient; at other times, you may need to work more closely with a particular student on his or her unique problems. Remember that if the student's self-esteem is not maintained or renewed, optimum learning will not occur. Try to boost your students' self-image by letting them know that they have capabilities and, when writing, that they have something to say worth reading. Showing that you care goes a long way toward motivating appropriate behavior. If you can get to know your students through their journals, do so. (For a discussion of journals in the developmental writing course, see Chapter 8 of this manual.) Remember unique things, such as a child's name, a pet, an upcoming birthday, or a particularly stressful situation the student has described. Besides merely writing notes to the students in their journals, casually ask about the child, pet, or situation. Knowing that you are truly interested in them can motivate students to attend class and do their assignments.

BE ORGANIZED. All developmental students appreciate and need an organized teacher. Whether or not you distribute a daily plan for the semester, you need to operate from one. Of course, you can always make changes, but having a schedule keeps you focused and keeps students aware of homework, writing assignments, and due dates. Students are more willing to attend classes when the instructors seem to know what they are doing and what they want to do.

EMPHASIZE THE COURSE'S BENEFITS. If, as is the case in many schools, your developmental course does not carry college credit, the students may decide that your class is not as important as, say, history or science. You may discover that students are skipping your class and neglecting your assignments to study for tests in other classes. When you know that students do so, talk to them and point out that the information and skills they will acquire in your class will help them in their credit classes. Begin the semester by illustrating how important writing is to success in history, psychology, science, and English classes—and in the students' future careers. If you can provide advice from your former students, do so. Call attention to the profiles in Chapter 1 of *Real Skills*. Incorporate real-world writing into your assignments. Once students can see connections among building their skills, the help that your course can offer, and their futures, you have a stronger chance of motivating them.

DO NOT GRADE EVERY ASSIGNMENT. One method of motivating students to revise papers is to avoid assigning a grade. A weak student may be satisfied with a low C, but if you put "Rewrite" at the top of the page instead of a grade, the student will feel obligated to revise and resubmit the paper. After students have done this for an assignment or two, they usually realize that it is easier to revise and edit on their own before they are instructed to do so by a teacher. You might also use red ink (the color most likely to get students' attention) to point out the paper's strengths.

ASK STUDENTS TO SET THEIR OWN GOALS. Another form of motivation requires the student's involvement in and commitment to his or her learning process. To encourage such active involvement, have students establish their own goals for the course and

them with you early in the term. At midterm,
the students look at those goals and write a
to you about why they are or are not reaching
n. Respond to each note in order to let the stu-
ts know if they are on target and to offer advice
ey are not.

As you attempt to motivate your students,
p in mind that a teacher can open the door but
student must go through alone; the first thing
at education should teach someone is how to
lk alone. Thus, remember that no matter what
otivational techniques you use, they will not al-
ays work. If the student is overwhelmed by other
lasses, work, family problems, or other distrac-
ons, what you do may not matter. As teachers we
ave to realize that we are not responsible for our
tudents' total successes or failures; too many fac-
ors are beyond our (or sometimes their) control.

Handling Rude and Disruptive Students

Nothing is more disconcerting than having to rep-
rimand students who should act like and be treated
as adults. Sometimes classmates will handle rudeness or disruption for you by asking those who are
out of line to be quiet or telling them to "grow up."
However, if you can keep the situation from reaching that point, everyone will be happier.

Keeping students busy probably does the best
job of prevention. If you have the class constantly
doing something different, then the potential troublemakers do not have as much time to act up. If you
are going over exercises and you have talkers, keep
calling on those talkers. Merely rotate through the
group, calling one name after another. Usually, the
remainder of the class catches on before they do,
but when they discover what you are doing, they
will generally calm down and cooperate to keep
from being singled out for answers.

If the problem is not solved by any of the techniques suggested above, take the offenders aside
and talk to them privately. Explain to them that
even if they believe the material being covered in
class is too easy or not important, most of their
classmates believe otherwise. Emphasize that they
are disturbing their classmates and keeping them
from learning. Most of the time, students will react
favorably if they realize they are disturbing their
peers rather than their teacher.

Rudeness must be dealt with swiftly before it
ruins the class atmosphere. At the first sign of rudeness, stop the class immediately; make it clear—

the first time—that you will not tolerate such behavior. Then, in a one-on-one conversation, try to
discover why the student was acting rudely. Some
students are rude and disruptive because they do
not believe they belong in a developmental English
class. If that is the case, calmly explain the school's
placement policy and tell them how better prepared
they will be for freshman composition after taking
your developmental class.

If students are rude to you, tell them that you
will all be happier and they will learn more if you
treat each other with respect. If they are rude to
students who are progressing slowly, ask them to
be patient. Explain that everyone in the class has
his or her own problems. You might even preempt
or subvert rudeness by asking students to assist
their classmates, pointing out that because there is
only one of you, you would certainly appreciate any
help they can give you.

Latecomers are a totally different issue. Some
teachers exhibit a low tolerance for tardiness,
whereas others do not let latecomers disturb them
outwardly. Many developmental students have so
many personal problems and obligations that they
have difficulty arriving at school on time. Weather
conditions, road construction, traffic accidents, and
car trouble may affect anyone. However, you must
make your standards known at the beginning of the
semester, checking to make sure that your school
will stand behind whatever you propose. For instance, some teachers lock the door when it is time
for class to begin, but some schools do not allow
students to be locked out of their classrooms. If
your school has an attendance policy, you may be
able to count a certain number of tardinesses as an
absence. You could also give a brief in-class activity or test at the beginning of each period. If the
student is on time, he or she gets credit. If the student is late, his or her grade suffers. Personally, although I want students to be on time, I prefer late
arrivals to total absences.

When handling rude or disruptive students, be
aware of your own attitudes or misconceptions. We
often dismiss difficult behavior and weak performance as stemming from the student's poor attitude.
However, we must consider the possibility that
many students have lived through years of failure
and frustration arising from conditions beyond
their control. Some have serious emotional or
learning disabilities. Such students have difficulty
with reading, writing, spelling, organizing their
thoughts and their lives, following instructions, or
staying on task for a reasonable length of time. In
addition, they often cause us frustration because

they can perform well on occasion. By talking to students one-on-one, you may discover individuals who want to learn but do not know how, or who are afraid to try for fear of more failure.

A Final Word

Teaching developmental students is a challenge, but the challenge is definitely worth it. Remember Anthony, the student who slept through his first class? He is the type of student who makes all the frustrations disappear, the kind who gears you up for the next semester. Three months after missing his first class, Anthony wrote his last journal entry of the semester:

> This is my last entry, and I really want to thank you for being a great teacher. You are very good at your job. I think you go out of your way for us. In fact, I know you do. You've helped me a lot and what I've learned will be a benefit to my life. I promise I won't give up or quit. I want something out of life, a future to contribute to my family and to my people so someone can see there is hope. I know if I apply myself I can make it. You let me know at the first day of school that I could do it. So thank you for your support and teaching.

4

Bringing the Real World into the Classroom

All learners learn best when they can see connections between the material to be mastered and their own goals, needs, and interests. By bringing the real world—whether that means college, work, or everyday life—into the developmental writing course, you will be demonstrating such connections. Students will see that writing is important to real life and necessary to what they want to accomplish in their own lives. This strategy will prove especially effective with older students, who are typically pragmatic and goal oriented and who have already been immersed in the real world outside the classroom.

That students often think of the writing course as a strictly academic subject is ironic, given the status of writing as an essential workplace skill. There is no professional occupation that does not require writing skills and almost no employer who would not be eager to promote someone with good analytical and communications skills. As stated in *Workplace Basics*, a summary of research conducted under a two-year joint project of the American Society for Training and Development and the U.S. Department of Labor, "Basic academic skills—reading, writing, and computation—have long been revered as the keys to success in society and the workplace. . . . [W]riting is frequently the first step in communicating with customers, interacting with machines, documenting competitive transactions, or successfully moving new ideas into the workplace."

The importance of the real world to students and the importance of writing in the real world are central assumptions at work on every page of *Real Skills*.

The following sections present some ways that you can integrate the real world into your course and some hints for using the corresponding features and sections in *Real Skills*.

Allow Students to See Themselves in the Course

Incorporating the real world into your classroom does not necessarily mean focusing on politics or writing-across-the-curriculum topics. The first and perhaps most important connection to the real world is the connection to each student. Students should see themselves reflected in course materials, content, assignments, and policies. They should know that the course is *about them*.

Whenever possible, encourage students to interject information about their own lives and experiences into discussions and activities. Ask them to write about things that they find useful or interesting. (You may want to use the Survey of Interests form in Chapter 5 of this instructor's manual to learn more about your students' interests.) Ask them to make connections between a rhetorical concept and their lives outside the classroom. Also, let students know that you value and respect them as developing writers. Display samples of their writing in the classroom, or assemble finished pieces in a class publication. Share the works of other student writers with them.

Student voices are a central part of Chapter 1 of *Real Skills*, in which several and current and former students provide advice for college success. Finally, the editing exercises at the end of the grammar chapter cover topics relevant to college, work, and everyday life to engage students.

Use Content from the Real World

Whether selecting content for reading, writing, or grammar practice, consider how well it reflects the world that your students experience outside the classroom. *Real Skills* is filled with examples intended to remind students of their real lives, whether that means college, work, or everyday life. Once you get into the habit, it is fairly easy to maintain this focus, but here are a few ideas to get you started.

COLLEGE

Content related to the majors your students are studying, such as

— Business

— Secretarial/office administration

— Accounting

— Nursing

— Health and human services

— Medical technician/dental technician

— Education

— Criminal justice

— Computers/electronics

— Manufacturing

— Automotive technician

— Agriculture

Financial aid

Racism and sexism on campus: discrimination, assault, official policies (including affirmative action)

Smoking policies

Drinking on campus

Parking on campus

Day care on campus

Academic advising and other support systems for students

Student lounge, other hangouts: how they should be changed, why they are good, why they are a waste of space or money

The registration process

What is a good student? What kind of student do they want to be?

Study aids: how to study, how to get an A, how to juggle course commitments

Access to computers and other technology

WORK

Finding a promising job

Writing a résumé

Preparing for interviews

Interacting with boss and colleagues

Learning new skills

Developing a career plan/career goals

Negotiating a promotion or salary increase

Exploring content related to the occupations your students typically have or go into

EVERYDAY LIFE

Parenting

Relationships

Friends

Drinking/drugs

Self-improvement

Planning, goal setting

Breaking bad habits

Juggling home, school, and work

Hobbies

Crime

Consumer goods

Local industries

Setting and managing a family budget

Health threats/natural disasters

Technology

Terrorism

Whenever possible, you might want to find examples from the local newspaper or from magazines that your students are most interested in to illustrate points you are making. You can find examples of rhetorical strategies or of different grammatical or stylistic approaches. Better yet, you can have your students search for the examples. It is especially informative when they find mistakes or examples that do not follow your rules. Such examples provide excellent opportunities for discussions of different styles and different interpretations of rules.

Use Real-World Assignments

Be sure to introduce real-world writing topics of your own. Use situations straight from the news for writing topics. Have students find classified ads for jobs that they might want and write letters of application. Or ask them to write a letter to another teacher asking for a change of grade.

You can also create more full-blown real-world scenarios. Choose a current issue, local or national, that your students should be aware of. Gather statistics, newspaper articles, brochures, pie charts, photographs, and any other materials that can help students understand the situation. Create players or groups of players, assign roles, and let students work in groups to plan their strategy. Then, you can spend one class period having the class act out the situation.

For instance, you can use the issue of threats against abortion clinics and even the murders of some of their personnel. Locally, you may have experienced abortion-related protests and minor conflicts. Therefore, your question for consideration might be "What can we do locally to try to prevent the possibility of violence?" For groups, you could identify pro-life advocates, pro-choice advocates (such as Planned Parenthood personnel), local law enforcement officials, medical professionals (doctors and nurses), and representatives of the local governing body. Groups of students would need to examine the data and decide on a position statement. Then they would develop logical arguments to present their viewpoints. One group will be responsible for calling a meeting, determining how the meeting will be conducted, and appointing a moderator to direct the meeting and bring it to a close. During the meeting, the various groups will present their arguments so that everyone has a chance to speak and to hear all sides of the issue. The class should try to come to a logical conclusion.

The following writing assignments can be derived from such an activity:

- One journal entry on topic before assignment is given, a second during the process, and a third to determine if attitudes have changed

- A position statement with logical arguments from each group

- A letter to the editor stating the student's opinion on the issue

- A response to a letter to the editor that was sympathetic to the violent protesters

- A journal entry from the perspective of a doctor or nurse who was threatened

- A journal entry from the perspective of a woman who has had an abortion

- A journal entry from the perspective of a protester who was arrested

- A proposal to the town's governing body recommending certain actions

- An editorial examining how far someone should take a moral commitment

- A paragraph detailing the government's role in mediating or defusing such situations

Another interesting situation would be a proposal to legalize casino gambling. Students could represent churches, politicians, social service organizations, residents, businesses that cater to tourists, law enforcement officials, and casino operators. Other controversial topics include allowing cities or towns to fly the Confederate flag; planning a drug rehabilitation facility in a residential neighborhood; building a Wal-Mart next to an upscale residential area; reforming welfare or finding ways to prevent violence in schools, beach erosion, or terrorism. The list of topics for simulation games is unlimited.

Send Students
Out of the Classroom

Create assignments that take your students outside the classroom and help them see how important writing is to success in the real world. You might have them write to an audience other than you, especially if their writing will help them accomplish something that they authentically want. For example, the class could collaborate in writing and sending (to the appropriate person on campus) a proposal for better parking facilities, improved curriculum standards, or more support services.

Another idea is to have students use their developing writing skills to help someone else. Investigate whether there are social service organizations in your community that need reporters or letter writers, and see if you can arrange for students to get credit for this work.

Students can also benefit from learning more about how writing is used in the careers they are looking forward to—as well as learning more about these careers in general. Ask students to interview someone who has a job they themselves would like to have. (They can use the sample Interview Guide on p. 47.)

Interview Guide for an Informational Interview

Use your interview guide to ask questions. Take notes on the person's answers, but do not forget to listen. Ask additional questions that occur to you during the interview.

Date of interview:

Name of person:

Company:

Position:

1. What are the major job responsibilities? (You may also want to ask for specific examples of tasks.)

   _____

   _____

   _____

   _____

2. What skills are necessary to do the job?

   _____

   _____

3. What prior experience is necessary or useful?

   _____

   _____

4. Describe an average day on the job.

   _____

   _____

   _____

5. What have you learned on the job?

    _____

    _____

6. What kind of person does well in the job?

    _____

    _____

7. What do people find interesting or like about the job?

    _____

    _____

8. What do people find frustrating or dislike about the job?

    _____

    _____

9. What kind of writing do you do in an average week? How important is writing to your job?

    _____

    _____

    _____

    _____

10. What advice would you give to someone who is interested in this type of work?

    _____

    _____

One interesting writing situation is to pair your class with a class from a local middle or junior high school. A class of sixth- or seventh-graders would benefit from knowing about the life experiences and challenges of many of your remedial students, and your students will have real-life readers.

Bring the Real World into the Classroom

Consider inviting a speaker into your class. A guest can provide a nice change of pace as well as give students a glimpse into life outside the classroom. Think about the kind of information your students need. If you teach at a two-year college, invite a counselor or the registrar to talk about transferring to a four-year school. Ask the financial aid director to discuss grants and scholarships. Arrange for a librarian to give your class an orientation to the library and to library research. Other college personnel can let your students know what kinds of services are available to students.

Perhaps some of your colleagues could talk about career opportunities in their fields. You could also invite local businesspeople to visit. They can offer advice on applying for jobs and writing résumés, or they could describe what they look for in an employee. Better yet, ask some former students to visit. They can tell your current students about the kind of writing they are doing in upper-level courses or on the job. Every visit can be followed by some type of writing assignment, either for a grade or for practice.

5

Integrating Critical Thinking into the Course

Chet Meyers, Metropolitan State University

Teaching writing and teaching critical thinking go hand in hand. *Real Skills* makes this partnership manageable. Even at the most fundamental level, the writing skills of sound paragraph and essay structure, organized and thoughtful presentation of support, and careful editing form the basis for more sophisticated critical thinking skills. You need not have two texts or two approaches in order to foster critical thinking in your developmental writing students. *Real Skills* encourages these students, who often have difficulty seeing themselves as thinkers and as writers, to *think like writers*. This section of *Practical Suggestions* offers you an overview of critical thinking (as educators have defined it in the past thirty years or so) and gives some concrete applications and activities for the classroom.

Critical thinking begins with a strong foundation of skills, content/knowledge, and attitudes. Because the interplay of these three factors is so crucial, a general framework for thinking about critical thinking can help teachers examine their teaching practice and explore how to encourage sound thinking in the teaching of writing. The framework that follows summarizes some of the major themes and issues that have characterized the critical thinking movement since the late 1970s.

Three Ways of Thinking about Critical Thinking

SKILLS. During the late 1970s and early 1980s, critical thinking in college and university teaching was generally associated with formal or informal logic, or with various approaches to problem solv-

ing. The assumption was that if we could teach students generic critical thinking skills, they could then apply those skills to any discipline. To some extent that has proved true. The more or less commonsense tools of inference, deduction, and sound argumentation illustrate basic reasoning skills that cut across all disciplines. However, a student who masters a course in informal logic or problem solving may need further practice to apply those skills to, say, art appreciation or college algebra.

CONTENT/KNOWLEDGE. A second approach, advocated by John McPeck in *Critical Thinking and Education* (1981), suggests that we consider how critical thinking necessarily varies among different disciplines. It does seem obvious that an artist goes about critical thinking differently than does a physicist. Likewise, a physicist's critical thinking abilities differ somewhat from those of a historian. The differences are natural, given the different assumptions these disciplines make about the nature of reality and their different ways of knowing. Most of us can relate to this personally. We have the ability to think critically about some subjects and yet remain baffled by others. Training in critical thinking involves practice in asking critical questions so that the physics student learns to think like a physicist, the history student learns to think like a historian, and the writing student learns to think like a writer.

ATTITUDES. A third approach to critical thinking grew out of the combined work of developmental psychologists such as Jean Piaget, William Perry, and Carol Gilligan and educators such as Steven Brookfield and Mary Field Belenky. The argument

here is that, in Piaget's terminology, our mental structures (the ways we organize our thinking processes) develop more or less naturally and become more sophisticated as we mature. As children encounter increasingly complex life problems, their mental structures become more sophisticated. Although there is still disagreement among developmental theorists and educators about the exact nature of these stages of development (particularly differences between men and women), there is overriding agreement that thinking skills are linked to ego development. And that suggests that cognitive skills are intimately tied to affective attitudes and, as Richard Paul wisely suggests in his book *Critical Thinking: What Every Person Needs to Survive in a Rapidly Changing World,* to moral development (255). Thus, students are more likely to advance intellectually in supportive and nurturing environments and where attitudes such as encouragement, open-mindedness, risk taking, appreciation of complexity, and collaborative learning are fostered.

If we consider these three approaches not as competing ideologies but as each having something worthwhile to contribute to the teaching of critical thinking, we can create a simple framework that can help us build a foundation for critical thinking in writing.

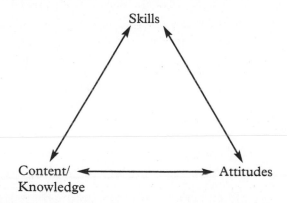

With this historical framework in mind, we can now consider the practical implications of these three different approaches to critical thinking and how we can use them to formulate an approach to teaching that will help students improve their thinking abilities.

Implications for Teaching and Learning

SKILLS. Students need to develop basic cognitive skills, some of which seem to come naturally and others of which need to be more explicitly taught. Teaching developmental writing should involve fostering students' analytical and evaluative skills as well. Many of the steps in the writing process for a paragraph or an essay—exploring and narrowing a topic, writing a topic sentence, organizing information and creating a structure, supporting a main point with details and evidence, and revising and editing for clarity and coherence—involve critical thinking. Special features in *Real Skills* (see, for example, the writing checklists in Chapter 8) encourage students to analyze and evaluate their work.

CONTENT/KNOWLEDGE. Thinking skills do not exist in a vacuum. Students cannot write about a topic unless they know something about it. Good thinking grows out of a strong base of information and evidence. In teaching developmental writing, we cannot expect students to have extensive knowledge of any particular subject, but we are not starting from zero. We can begin by drawing on students' interests and life experiences, and then challenge them to explore those areas in more depth and with sophistication. Rather than assigning all students to write about the Declaration of Independence, begin with something that is already percolating in their minds. Allowing variety in topic selection, variety that appeals to different student interests, is a good starting place. To that end, I have included a simple Survey of Interests form (see p. 53), which you may consider distributing at the beginning of the first class. Use this tool to discover what students really might want to write about and to collect an initial writing sample.

ATTITUDES. Students will develop good thinking skills in an environment that both challenges and supports them. The best critical thinkers are individuals who have some sense of their own worth and who have experienced success in their undertakings. Open-mindedness, risk taking, persistence, inquisitiveness, the humility to admit mistakes, and the courage to start over do not develop in an oppressive and punitive atmosphere. I cannot stress strongly enough the role of the teacher as coach and cheerleader. The best teachers know how to combine discipline and rigor with support and encouragement. Indeed, the general atmosphere in the classroom is often one of the best indicators of whether or not critical thinking is being encouraged. If students are actively engaged—discussing, laughing, arguing, or even quietly pondering—it is a good bet they are developing sound thinking abilities. (See the *Instructor's Annotated Edition of Real Skills* for suggested collaborative activities and discussion tips.) In contrast, in those neatly ordered, rows-all-straight-and-tidy classrooms where the teacher is front and center presenting information and where students always sit passively jotting down a note or two, there is little encouragement for the development of good thinking abilities.

Tips for Fostering Active, Critical Learning

Teaching skills, content/knowledge, and attitudes in a developmental writing course may sound like heaping just so many more expectations on already burdened instructors. That need not be the case. But to alleviate the supposed burden, some of us do need to rethink what teaching is about and focus our attention on *learning*. Thirty years ago we knew much less about the exact nature of the learning process than we do today. The old model of teacher-as-lecturer and student-as-note-taker was firmly rooted in the assumption that the teacher's job was to *transmit* knowledge to the student. Students were regarded as empty vessels waiting to be filled by wise and knowledgeable teachers. Today, we know that that old model has very limited efficacy. Indeed, most recent studies by educational psychologists and cognitive scientists argue that learning is less about receiving knowledge than it is about constructing knowledge. In the words of Jean Piaget, "children do not receive knowledge passively but rather discover and construct knowledge through activities" (119). That means we need to take more time in our classes for students to en-

gage in activities that will help them formulate new mental structures to serve as the building blocks for critical thinking (Meyers 13). Numerous studies have shown that when traditional lecturing is compared with more active forms of teaching and learning, in the context of general retention and practical learning outcomes, active learning almost always wins out—hands down (Erickson; Bransford; Kolb; Pollio).

So critical thinking and active learning are inextricably linked. The trick is to learn how to structure our classes so that active learning becomes a regular part of the teaching/learning process that both teachers and students can enjoy. What follows are four rather simple suggestions that can serve as a guide to creating a classroom that fosters critical thinking. (For additional suggestions, see Chapter 8 of this manual.)

ENCOURAGE STUDENT INTERACTION. When Fortune 500 executives spend hundreds of thousands of dollars for consultants to help them arrange office furniture in optimal ways to enhance employee interaction, you know American business is on to something. In the real world of work, a dynamic and flexible physical environment enhances employee productivity. It is unfortunate that some college classrooms—where students prepare for work—still have desks bolted to the floor. "Unbolting" the desks is the first step in encouraging shared inquiry, collaboration, and critical problem solving.

There are many different ways to arrange classroom furniture to encourage interaction. Desks can be placed in a horseshoe shape, with the opening toward the writing board. An ideal arrangement for a writing class is to place tables and chairs in a modified diamond shape, with four or five chairs at each table. One advantage of tables is that students can work in small groups. Many college writing programs stress a small-group approach to the teaching of developmental writing. A class might begin with a brief presentation by the teacher on paragraph construction, followed by illustrations from a few models. Next, students work individually on a paragraph and then meet as a group to share their writing and to receive helpful feedback. Of course, good small-group interaction needs to be modeled and ground rules for interaction must be laid down (see Chapter 6 in this manual), but the activity of students working with each other is a powerful stimulation to learning. The key here is to structure small-group activities for optimal productivity (see Johnson, Johnson, and Smith).

overhead

writing board

Modified diamond-shape arrangement facing the teacher and writing board

ALLOW MORE TIME FOR STUDENT–TEACHER AND STUDENT–STUDENT INTERACTION. Perhaps the most difficult aspect of helping students develop their own critical thinking skills is the need for teachers to move from center stage. The best teachers of critical thinking in any discipline are those who see their role as chief choreographer, not lead actor. There is very little that we lecture on that cannot be conveyed by means of some other, more engaging method.

Although brief mini-lectures provide a good way to focus attention and to set the agenda for the day, most time in class should be focused on student activities: sharing and critiquing papers, group editing, learning how to provide helpful feedback, or working on other small-group tasks. Once active learning becomes a regular part of the teaching–learning process, students remain focused, and instead of fidgeting ten minutes before class ends, they often have difficulty disengaging from their small-group activities. They will become more goal oriented and less concerned with the clock.

TO GET CLASS STARTED, CONSIDER BRIEF ACTIVITIES. The key to sound classroom activities is inciting student interest. Presenting activities and content in a real-world, familiar context is a productive

start. You can design successful, interesting class openers around a short reading and problem-solving exercises that build basic reading and writing skills. Consider the following options, and see Chapter 8 of this manual for more suggestions for active learning.

Students enter class and sit at tables with four or five chairs. You direct them to read Rob Bermingham's "Illusion of Privacy" in the Readings section of *Real Skills*. It will take about ten minutes to read the guiding question and the essay. Ask students to (1) summarize the main point of the essay in one or two sentences, (2) cite with a direct quote one of the reasons that people should be wary what they post online, and (3) list some possible ways to address the problem. Students spend another ten minutes writing their individual responses to these questions, and then they collaborate to see if they can build a consensus answer. You then solicit a response from each group to build a classwide consensus. The entire exercise takes about twenty-five minutes and can provide a jump start for a longer writing assignment. Skills involved in this exercise include reading, reflecting, summarizing, seeking evidence, analyzing, drawing one's own conclusions, talking and listening to others, and synthesizing to build consensus.

Second, consider circulating a short paragraph that needs editing. Each of the grammar chapters in *Real Skills* ends with paragraph-editing practices that you can use for this activity. Ask students to spend five minutes editing the piece individually and to work for another five or ten minutes in a small group to come up with their best editing suggestions. Then, ask each group to report back while you use an overhead projector to explore options and illustrate the class's final editing suggestions.

Finally, you may want to use one or more of the critical thinking activities provided at the end of this chapter. Each of these provides a critical thinking warm-up for the rest of the day's activities and helps to promote active, critical learning. You may spend five or ten minutes discussing how the skills involved in the various critical thinking activities apply to the writing process.

ALLOW QUIET TIME FOR REFLECTION. The hustle and bustle of an active-learning classroom is contagious and does a lot to stimulate thinking abilities, but so does quiet time. Different students learn in different ways. Some are more reflective than others; and no matter what their learning style, all students need some quiet time for the brain to process and incorporate new learning. In John

Dewey's words, "All reflection involves, at some point, stopping external observation and reactions so that an idea may mature" (210).

A problem here is that most teachers are very uncomfortable with silence in the classroom. Studies of what is referred to as "wait time"—the time between when a teacher asks a question and, seeing no response, either calls on a student or volunteers his or her own answer—suggest that teachers wait only about as long as it takes a butterfly to flap its wings once, or 0.9 seconds ("Slow Down You Move Too Fast"). Time for reflection can be built into writing exercises and problem-solving exercises or made a part of the teacher's open queries to the class. "What do you think the main problem with this paragraph structure is?" PAUSE . . . PAUSE . . . and more PAUSE. When we do take time to slow down and allow our students the luxury of a few moments of silence in the classroom, some wonderful things can happen. Students who never spoke before might volunteer, or we might find a student's answer challenges our own interpretations, allowing us also to experience the gift of new learning. Our purpose is to foster an environment where students can think critically, not quickly.

Developing Writing Assignments That Promote Critical Thinking

It is important to remember that learning to think critically does not happen overnight. The nature of teaching critical thinking in writing requires a building-block process that starts with simple assignments and progresses to higher levels of thinking. Here are some tips you may find helpful in designing effective writing assignments.

SEQUENCE ASSIGNMENTS TO BUILD SKILLS. Sequencing assignments to build from basic to more sophisticated cognitive skills enables you to observe student progress and allows students the opportunity for practice and, in turn, increased confidence. *Real Skills* offers carefully sequenced assignments: In Chapter 8, students move through the rhetorical methods from narration to argument, and within Chapter 8 of Part Two and the readings at the end of the book, students read and analyze example paragraphs before writing their own. Consider beginning with narration or illustration, which involve thinking abilities such as sorting through information, providing examples, organizing key details and events, and summarizing. Beyond that, ask

students to spend some time writing comparison/contrast paragraphs, which involve analytical thinking. You might then progress to argument paragraphs, which require students to recognize and counter assumptions. Throughout the process of any writing assignment, encourage students to ask a series of critical questions. By sequencing assignments that build from basic cognitive skills to higher-level thinking, we can help students become more aware of the role that critical thinking plays in writing.

DRAW ON STUDENTS' REAL-LIFE AND WORK EXPERIENCES. Another consideration in creating writing assignments is to develop them on the basis of our students' real-world interactions. The deathly prose that too often characterizes student papers often results from the "already dead" subjects they are asked to write about. Consider using the Survey of Interests form provided in this chapter, or one that you create on your own. Nothing enlivens writing more than assigning topics that are already fermenting in students' minds. Providing a real-world context helps to build critical thinking and writing skills. Issues being debated on your campus—tuition hikes, placement testing, or student parking, for example—can all serve as grist for the writing mill. The assignments throughout *Real Skills* have been constructed to reflect as accurately as possible students' real academic, work, and personal experiences.

A note about giving instructions for writing assignments: I cannot overemphasize the importance of being clear and unambiguous. We may know what we mean when we ask students to *summarize, evaluate,* or *analyze,* but students do not always know. *Analyze,* perhaps the most overused word in college assignments, may have many different meanings for students: "compare similarities or differences," "respond to personally," or "debate." Be clear in your definition of words such as *summary, evaluation,* and *analysis.* You may want to ask students to define these words and describe what kind of thinking each requires. Then, measure their responses against your own expectations for individual writing assignments. Carefully consider the types of thinking, as well as the types of rhetorical development, that you want students to practice in each writing assignment.

There are many ways writing teachers can help their students build a strong foundation for critical thinking. The challenge is to trust that students do, in fact, have the ability to begin thinking critically, if we will only provide a foundation and a context, and then get out of the way and allow them time in class to practice and develop those abilities. Stepping down from the podium does not mean relinquishing all control. But becoming a good choreographer for student learning will require us to rethink our role as teacher. There are some losses in no longer being the center of attention. The gains, however, are considerable when we see the progress our students make and know that we helped point them in the direction of active, critical learning.

Critical Thinking Activities

On the pages that follow are a variety of activities that promote critical and creative thinking:

- *Think Again* activities are logic puzzles that students must solve by abandoning conventional lines of thought and uncovering new possibilities.

- *Figure It Out* activities are visual puzzles that require students to deduce rules from a set of statements and then to articulate the rules in clear definitions.

- *Focus—and Refocus* activities are also visual, but as in the Think Again activities, students must solve them by reconsidering assumptions and finding unconventional perspectives.

- *Conundrums* are exercises in logical deduction—with a creative twist.

All activities but the Conundrums can be photocopied and distributed to students for either independent or group work. These activities work well as icebreakers or to introduce collaboration. The Conundrums are meant to be read aloud and worked on by the class as a whole (or by a smaller group) as a collaborative, in-class activity.

The solution for each Think Again, Figure It Out, and Focus—and Refocus activity is printed on the back of the page, so you can either copy and distribute these as well or simply let students know what the answers are. Encourage students to challenge answers they find faulty or to defend alternative solutions. By analyzing and discussing the assumptions and logic of each puzzle, students will greatly increase their abilities to think critically and creatively.

Think Again

Set A

Sometimes you need to look at a problem from a new perspective to see the solution. Try some creative thinking to solve these puzzles.

1. Two plumbers were working together on a new apartment building. One of them was the father of the other one's son. How is this possible?

2. What five-letter word becomes shorter when you add two letters to it?

3. Tom has two younger sisters who each want him to take her to the movies. Tom also has a limited budget. Would it be cheaper for him to take his sisters to see a movie together, to take them each separately, or doesn't it matter?

4. A king has promised his kingdom to whichever of his two children has the *slower* horse, and he starts them on a race to the most distant city in the realm. Because neither of them wants to arrive first, the prince and the princess meander slowly around the kingdom for weeks. Finally, they meet an old villager who proposes a solution, and the prince and the princess are soon racing as fast as they can to the distant city. What is the villager's solution?

Set B

Sometimes you need to look at a problem from a new perspective to see the solution. Try some creative thinking to solve these puzzles.

1. An airplane flying off the coast of southern California has as its two passengers two men trying to settle a bet. One of them has bet the other that if he drops a one-pound brick out of the plane ten seconds after the other man has dropped a one-pound sack of cotton out of the plane, the brick will hit the ground first. Which of the two will actually hit the ground first?

2. A careless driver drove his truck under an overpass that was not quite high enough to let the truck through. He was stuck tight and could drive neither forward nor backward. Finally, he came up with a way to get his truck unstuck. How did he do it?

3. Two mothers and two daughters were fishing, and they each caught a fish. But only three fish were caught. How is this possible?

Think Again

Answers for Set B

These are the answers that we had in mind. If you came up with something different, though, you might just have a different perspective.

Answer for 1. Neither. If the plane is flying off the coast of southern California, they will both hit the water.

Answer for 2. The truck driver let some of the air out of his tires.

Answer for 3. There were only three people fishing: a grandmother, a mother, and a daughter. The mother is both a mother and a daughter.

Figure It Out

Pringles

Imagine you are learning a new language and are shown the objects below. Some are called *pringles* and some are not, but it is difficult at first to figure out exactly what makes an object a *pringle*. Analyze the objects to find out what the *pringles* have in common; keep in mind that there may be other *pringles* than the ones you see here.

When you have figured out what makes an object a *pringle*, write a clear definition here:

To be a *pringle,* an object must _____

_____

_____

This is a pringle.

This is a pringle.

This is not a pringle.

This is a pringle.

This is not a pringle.

This is not a pringle.

Figure It Out

Answer for Pringles

This is the answer that we had in mind. If you came up with something different, though, you might just have a different perspective.

To be a *pringle,* an object must _____ **be a shape with sides of equal length.** _____

_____

Laracks

Imagine you are learning a new language and are shown the objects below. Some are called *laracks* and some are not, but it is difficult at first to figure out exactly what makes an object a *larack*. Analyze the objects to find out what the laracks have in common; keep in mind that there may be other *laracks* than the ones you see here.

When you have figured out what makes an object a *larack*, write a clear definition here:

To be a *larack*, an object must _____

_____

This is a larack.

This is not a larack.

This is not a larack.

This is a larack.

This is a larack.

This is not a larack.

Answer for Laracks

This is the answer that we had in mind. If you came up with something different, though, you might just have a different perspective.

To be a *larack*, an object must _____ be an eating utensil intended to hold liquid. _____

_____

Squares

To figure something out, sometimes we need to look beyond the obvious answers—and sometimes we need to consider the answers that we thought were *too* obvious to be important. Be sure to explore all the possibilities.

How many squares are in this picture?

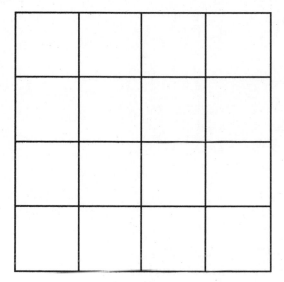

Answer for Squares

There are thirty squares.

Word Puns

To figure something out, sometimes we need to look beyond the obvious answers—and sometimes we need to consider the answers that we thought were *too* obvious to be important. Be sure to explore all the possibilities.

What does each of these mean?

1. $\dfrac{\text{STAND}}{\text{I}}$ = _____

2. /READING/ = _____

3. T = _____
   O
   U
   C
   H

4. $\dfrac{\text{MAN}}{\text{BOARD}}$ = _____

5. LIFE/THE = _____

6. ECNALG = _____

Focus—and Refocus

Answers for Word Puns

1. $\dfrac{\text{STAND}}{\text{I}}$ = _____ I understand _____

2. /READING/ = _____ reading between the lines _____

3. T = _____ touchdown _____
    O
    U
    C
    H

4. $\dfrac{\text{MAN}}{\text{BOARD}}$ = _____ man overboard _____

5. LIFE/THE = _____ the afterlife _____

6. ECNALG = _____ backwards glance _____

Lines

To figure something out, sometimes we need to look beyond the obvious answers—and sometimes we need to consider the answers that we thought were *too* obvious to be important. Be sure to explore all the possibilities.

Can you draw a line through each of these dots, without lifting your pencil and by making only three turns (for a total of four straight segments)? You can only go through each dot once.

```
•      •      •


•      •      •


•      •      •
```

Answer for Lines

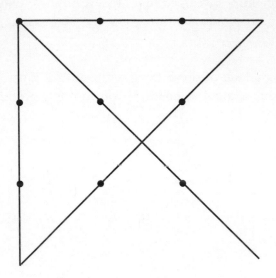

Conundrums

Note to Instructor: These are meant to be used for collaborative in-class activities, not treated as handouts. You (or a student) should act as the presenter and read a scenario out loud; the presenter should know what the solution is. The students listening should take on the role of detectives and work together to find the solution. The detectives can ask the presenter any question that can be answered with a yes or a no, and the presenter must answer truthfully.

SCENARIO 1
A woman walks into a restaurant and asks for a drink. The waitress quickly pulls out a gun and points it at her. The woman says "thank you" and leaves. What happened?

SOLUTION 1
The woman had hiccups. The waitress frightened her and helped her get rid of them.

SCENARIO 2
A man is afraid to go home because there is a man with a mask there. What is going on?

SOLUTION 2
The man is playing baseball and is on third base; the man with the mask is the catcher, who has the ball.

SCENARIO 3
A guard walks in and finds a prisoner has hanged himself, using the fabric from his shirt to make a noose and stringing it over a hook in the ceiling. The man's feet dangle three feet off the floor, but there is no furniture in the cell and nothing but the floor to stand on. How did the man hang himself?

SOLUTION 3
There is a puddle of water on the floor. The man stood on a block of ice, which has now melted.

SCENARIO 4
In the middle of the Mediterranean Sea is a large yacht with several corpses floating nearby. What happened?

SOLUTION 4
The passengers decided to go swimming, so they all dove into the water. However, they neglected to set up a ladder, so they couldn't get back into the yacht.

SCENARIO 5
Jake comes home to find broken glass and Ginger lying in a pool of water and broken glass. Although Ginger looks fine, he knows immediately that she is dead of suffocation. Why?

SOLUTION 5
Ginger is Jake's goldfish and her bowl has broken.

References

Bransford, J. *Human Cognition*. Belmont: Wadsworth, 1979. Print.

Dewey, John. *How We Think*. 1910. Lexington: Heath, 1982. Print.

Erickson, S. C. *The Essence of Good Teaching: Helping Students Learn and Remember What They Learn*. San Francisco: Jossey, 1984. Print.

Johnson, D., R. Johnson, and K. A. Smith. *Active Learning: Cooperation in the College Classroom*. Edina: Interaction, 1991. Print.

Kolb, David A. *Experiential Learning: Experience as a Source of Learning and Development*. Englewood Cliffs: Prentice, 1984. Print.

McPeck, John. *Critical Thinking and Education*. New York: St. Martin's, 1981. Print.

Meyers, Chet. *Teaching Students to Think Critically*. San Francisco: Jossey, 1986. Print.

Meyers, Chet, and Tom Jones. *Promoting Active Learning: Strategies for the College Classroom*. San Francisco: Jossey, 1993. Print.

Paul, Richard. *Critical Thinking: What Every Person Needs to Survive in a Rapidly Changing World*. Sonoma: Center for Critical Thinking, 1992. Print.

Piaget, Jean. *Psychology of Intelligence*. 1947. Totowa: Littlefield, 1976. Print.

Pollio, H. R. *What Students Think About and Do in College Lectures Classes*. Teaching and Learning Issues no. 53. Knoxville: Learning Research Center, U of Tennessee, 1984. Print.

"Slow Down You Move Too Fast." *Phi Delta Kappan* 69 (1987): 234. Print.

Whitehead, A. N. *The Aims of Education*. 1929. New York: Free Press, 1967. Print.

6

Facilitating Collaboration

Collaboration can range from a ten-minute group activity or session of peer editing to a collaborative writing project lasting for several weeks and involving a whole class. Whatever the exact configuration, students tend to benefit enormously. Most obvious, they gain writing skills: They get a better sense of their audience and how to shape writing to it; they improve their ability to identify and discuss various characteristics of writing; and they gain a deeper understanding of writing as a communicative (and social) process. They also learn to give and receive feedback, improving their interaction and communication skills, often with students who are quite different from them. And they learn the value of learning, evaluating, and incorporating other people's ideas and insights into their own work.

Instructors also benefit from collaboration. Final drafts that have been through the stage of peer editing are inevitably more thoughtfully developed and contain fewer surface errors than those that have not. And collaboration can help create a manageable dynamic in large classes: Instead of having to attend to twenty-five or thirty people at once, the instructor can focus on a few students at a time while the others are working with their peers.

Creating a Collaborative Environment

True collaborative work grows out of an environment in which all students feel valued and have the confidence they need to take risks. It is hard to establish this overnight, so the first group work of the semester may be a bit rocky, but here are some things to keep in mind.

GIVE STUDENTS SOMETHING REAL TO ACCOMPLISH. Like all other methods of active learning, collabo-

ration needs a real goal, a real purpose. Otherwise it is just seen as busywork, and rightly so. You do not have to grade collaborative work to let students know it is valued: Make it a necessary part of completing some larger project, and give them credit for accomplishing it.

GIVE STUDENTS CLEAR GUIDELINES. Be very clear about what you want students to accomplish (e.g., a brainstorming list with at least ten items, comments on all the paragraphs that the group members have brought to class); any requirements you have for how they should accomplish it (e.g., round-robin comments, debate, written comments); and how long they have. You may want to distribute checklists to make sure students answer all the questions you have for them. Giving them all the information they need up front will help them understand the ground rules and feel more in control. You may want to put key instructions on the board or on a handout.

GIVE STUDENTS OWNERSHIP OF THEIR OWN GROUPS. As far as you are comfortable with this, let students know that they are in charge of their own groups and how they operate. (You may want to go over some guidelines for treating one another with respect, if this is a concern for you.) Offer yourself as a resource, but not as a leader. In the beginning of the semester you may need to provide more guidance and models, but by the end of the semester, students should be able to work out rules for turn-taking and to assign roles (secretary, moderator, etc.) on their own.

ALLOW STUDENTS TO EXPERIMENT AND TO MAKE MISTAKES. One benefit of the collaborative process is that students often arrive at unpredictable answers or explanations that they would never have come up with on their own. In other words, your students will probably surprise you! You don't want students to jump on a runaway train and abandon the assignment altogether, but allowing them a little free rein will give them more confidence in their own creativity. You may also need to grant a little latitude toward groups that completely misunderstand some part of the assignment and go down the wrong path, especially early in the semester. Use it as an opportunity to discuss and refine the class's collaborative methods.

ENCOURAGE STUDENTS TO HELP ONE ANOTHER. Rather than jumping in with the answer whenever students have questions, encourage them to find other students to help them out—either within their groups (if they are currently working in groups) or among the students in the class as a whole. You will not have to answer the same questions over and over, students will feel freer to ask any questions they have, and the answer-givers will gain confidence in themselves as experts.

Forming Groups

Occasionally, a collaborative project is the product of a whole class's unified efforts, and sometimes a collaborative strategy requires students to work in pairs. But often the best collaborative configuration is the small group, which immediately leads to two questions: How small? and How are the groups determined?

For the most part, small groups of three to five students work well. If there are more than that, the group tends to plod along as everyone takes a turn—or else someone drops back and says nothing at all. If a class has been working in groups for the entire semester and has mastered the related skills, larger groups sometimes can be formed for the final project in the course.

There are a number of ways to put together groups, and all have advantages and disadvantages; the most important thing is for you to know what your goals are and to choose a method that suits you and your students.

TEACHER-SELECTED GROUPS. For the first group work of the course, you should probably establish the groups yourself. You can try putting like with like (nursing students together, older students together) to ease the social tension and establish camaraderie.

But try mixing things up a little, too: Do not allow any one group to be completely homoge-

neous, and make sure the better writers or good class participants are scattered throughout; weak students will benefit from working with stronger ones. And the point, after all, is to help students learn to work with people who are not necessarily like them.

RANDOM GROUPS. For a braver experiment, you can also assign students randomly to groups, having them pick numbers out of a hat, for example. This method has the advantage of appearing "fair" and may result in extremely productive groupings you would never have come up with on your own.

SELF-SELECTED GROUPS. You can also let students settle themselves into groups; as you might predict, friends will generally stick with friends, and all students will generally seek out others who seem like them. This technique has the advantage of easing the social interactions, but sometimes it is harder to get self-selected groups to settle down and work productively. The groups will tend to be uneven, as well, as all of the students of each type (ESL, slower students, faster students, those with the same major) congregate; and some students may feel left out or mismatched if you put them in a group in which they are the only outsiders. Generally, the disadvantages of this scheme can be overcome if you wait to let students choose their own groups until later in the semester, once they are used to working with their classmates.

Collaborative Activities

This section presents some ideas for collaborative activities and practices you can use in your classroom. When designing collaborative projects, keep in mind your goals, your comfort level, and your student population. Start small and build on your success.

The *Instructor's Annotated Edition of Real Skills* contains marginal notes labeled "Teamwork" that describe collaborative activities. Note also that almost every chapter of *Real Skills* includes collaborative activities (in the Practice Together section) aimed at engaging students with different learning styles.

Peer Evaluation

Some students may feel uncomfortable commenting on another student's paper because they lack confidence in their own abilities to evaluate writing. Emphasize that they are helping their class-mates before you read and grade the assignment. Also, remind them that they should know what they understand and what they do not, what seems clear and what does not. They know what interests them and what they want or need more information about. You can also tell them that it is easier to analyze and respond to a classmate's writing than to their own. However, after experiencing peer editing, they will start to reflect on their own writing and begin to see their own problems.

The following are suggestions for various forms of peer editing. In most cases, peer editing sessions will be more productive if there is a specific set of questions for readers to answer. Some suggestions are provided in *Real Skills*. Additionally, the *Student Center for Real Skills* at bedfordstmartins.com/realskills has peer-review guides for all the types of writing covered in Chapter 8 of the text.

PAIRS. In the simplest version of peer editing, students can be paired to read and comment on each other's writing assignments. The comments can be written or oral.

SMALL-GROUP EDITING. One student reads his or her paper to the group; then, the group offers comments and suggestions. So that the author can listen more completely, another member of the group can be assigned to write down the suggestions and comments.

In another variation, someone other than the writer can read the paper aloud so the writer can hear his or her words. If the reader stumbles over a certain area, the writer knows that the area needs to be edited.

CIRCLE EDITING. Circle editing is a great way to begin because all students are together with the instructor, who guides the discussion. All students are exposed to most of the writings in the classroom without having all comments made by one student or a small group of students.

Have students bring their drafts to class and have the class as a whole form a circle; you should be part of the circle, too. Make sure everyone has a hard surface on which to write and a colored pen for editing. Ask students to pass their papers to the right three times. Then, ask a specific question (Does the essay have a clearly stated main point? Does the writer provide adequate support for the main point?) and have each student write a response based on the paper in his or her hands. Then, have them pass the papers to the right and ask a

second question. Continue passing the essays around the circle, asking a different question each time.

SELECTED SAMPLE. This is another whole-class activity and is useful for modeling the response process. The instructor selects or asks for a volunteer and shows the student's draft on an overhead projector. The class can see the assignment on the screen, and all can comment on that particular author's work.

ASSESSMENT. Give the class a set of grading criteria. Show one or two sample paragraphs, and evaluate them as a class. Then, divide the class into groups and have them evaluate each other's assignments.

Group Projects

Although peer evaluation may account for the majority of collaborative projects in a writing class, you can select from any of the following ideas for drawing students together into a community of learners. All the ideas offer opportunities for a break from the traditional lecture and emphasize active learning in various stages of the writing process and in grammar study.

IN-CLASS BRAINSTORMING AND PLANNING. Many students have trouble getting started on an assignment, so you can help by having the entire class brainstorm, plan, and organize a paragraph. For instance, if you are beginning a comparison/contrast assignment, choose discussion topics that all students can relate to, such as fast-food restaurants. Then, you can ask students to compare and contrast two different eating places within easy access to the college. Walk the class through the process by writing (or having students write) responses on the board.

1. Brainstorm—listing various places. Then, have the class pick two, pointing out that they cannot just pick any two (e.g., McDonald's and Taco Bell do not offer the same kind of food).

2. Brainstorm—listing possible points of comparison and contrast.

3. Select the best points to discuss.

4. Decide on an approach: comparison, contrast, combination.

5. Write a topic sentence for a paragraph.

6. Decide on a point-by-point or whole-to-whole organization.

7. Complete the outline (either the list of points or topic sentences).

Chapter 8 of *Real Skills* includes outlines that you might use.

GROUP PARAGRAPH. For comparison/contrast writing, bring to class a few articles of clothing that are similar but that have obvious differences (e.g., different brands of sneakers, hats from different eras, or shirts of different fabrics). Divide the class into small groups, and give each group two items to compare. Ask one student to write a topic sentence for a paragraph and then pass the paper around for other students to write one sentence with details to support the topic sentence.

PAIR-WRITTEN PARAGRAPH. Divide students into teams, and assign each team a hands-on process such as popping corn or tying shoes. The teams then talk through the process, outline the process step by step, and then draft the paragraph.

TEXT RECONSTRUCTION. Take a model paragraph and scramble the sentences, then ask students to work independently to number the sentences in a logical order. Then, have them compare their arrangements in small groups and discuss differences with other students, explaining why they decided on that particular organization. Such an assignment helps students learn to read more critically and to focus on clues regarding the relationships between sentences. Thus, students become more aware of transitions and other cohesive devices in writing so that they can apply the concepts to their own writing.

GRAMMAR PRACTICE. Have students write a collaborative story with specific grammatical or stylistic requirements for each sentence. For example, ask each student to write a compound sentence that begins with "The vampire had a beautiful pair of fangs, but then . . ." Next, ask the students to pass the paper to the person behind them. Ask students to add a complex sentence containing a clause with the word *which*. Continue around the room until you have covered all the points you want to address.

GRAMMAR REVIEW. For a great review of all the grammar instruction your students have received, have students work in pairs to revise a packet of sentences. Depending on the amount of time you have, the packet can vary from one to six pages and take up one to several class sessions. Before the due date, each student takes his or her packet home to confirm a final version of each sentence. You can count the revised packet as a test grade.

7

Teaching with Technology

Revised by Sharon Gerald, Jones County Junior College

We no longer ask *if* we are going to use technology in the classroom; we only ask how. Technology permeates academic, professional, and personal lives. The immense popularity of social networking sites like MySpace, Facebook, and Twitter, along with netbooks, iPhones, Blackberries, Kindles, and other Internet gadgetry, means that writing via technology is simply a fact of life for one and all.

Regardless of major, regardless of the degree of academic preparation for college, all of our students need basic technological communications skills. This need presents a conundrum for faculty who may not have a technological background and may not always feel comfortable teaching with newer technologies. You do not have to be an expert, however, to find effective ways to use computer technologies in the classroom. You can learn some skills at the same time that your students learn them. In fact, announcing that you will be learning a new technology with your students helps them work past their own technological nervousness and gives them a cheerful model—we are all in this together. They gain even more confidence when they can answer a technical question you have instead of the other way around.

Just because incorporating technology is important does not mean that every technological advance that comes along is vital for your classroom. You will want to adopt technologies thoughtfully and selectively. They should complement the purpose of your course and your own teaching style. They should not distract from your interaction with your students. Technology is rarely a good substitute for personal instruction. Rather, it is a way to supplement and enhance your own best teaching.

As you sort out what technologies to use in your classroom, here are some ideas you might find helpful. You will also find ideas for computer use in the margins of the *Instructor's Annotated Edition of Real Skills.*

Word Processing

Not so long ago, we may have debated whether to have students type or handwrite. Those days are gone. Formal handwritten communication is a thing of the past. We assume students will use word processing as an integral part of writing.

The ability to create a typed, well-formatted paper is a basic literacy we expect students to achieve, and word processing programs make this easier to do. But when we look past the software's formatting defaults to what it does to support the full writing process, we see ways students can begin to brainstorm, plan, and draft directly from their computers, transforming them from mere typesetting tools into rich writing tools. For example, most students will more willingly revise and edit when they do not have to rewrite laboriously by hand. So computers can both save students time and help them improve the quality of their writing. Keep in mind, however, that although word processing programs include tools that can improve both writing and editing if used properly, even computer-savvy students need guided instruction in the use of these tools. So it helps to review a few basic concepts.

Spell checkers are useful writing aids. They can cut down on spelling errors significantly. Of course, spell checkers do not work for commonly confused words (*there, their, they're,* and so on). Spell checkers are also of limited value for students with learning disabilities manifested in their spelling or who are particularly poor spellers. The spell checker might not be able to give options for these students' extremely misspelled words, and when options do appear, the students might not know which one to choose. And sometimes a correctly spelled word might not be in the spell checker's dictionary, and so the checker might suggest an incorrect alternative for a correctly spelled word. Still, many students (and some faculty) find that spell checkers help them avoid spelling errors that significantly detract from the readability and polish of a piece of writing. Teach students how to look at the words being flagged, to look at the choices, and to make the right decisions about the spell checkers' recommendations. If correct words are being flagged as incorrect, for example, students can add them to their dictionaries.

Grammar checkers are useful but more problematic. They ask students to look at their sentences and consider them as units of grammar, which is all to the good. However, grammar checkers isolate sentences and thus pull them out of context. They look for patterns or formulas in word order and then tell users which passages do not fit the patterns. Remind students that computers cannot read or reason. The students themselves must analyze the sentences to determine which contain grammatical errors. Inevitably, grammar checkers have "false positives" that identify an error where there is none, and "false negatives" that fail to identify an error where there is one. Students who do not have great skill or confidence in their writing will find it difficult to evaluate the computer's advice, and certainly students do not learn much or guarantee their success by simply accepting whatever the computer suggests. Ask students to use the word processing software's highlighter to mark flagged sentences that they remain unsure about revising. You can collect those sentences and build editing or grammar revision labs around them because it is very likely those sentences will represent issues many of your students have. Remind students that grammar checkers are poor substitutes for their own sentence-by-sentence review and encourage them to consult their text—by looking up the grammar issue flagged in their table of contents or index—or to ask you or a writing center tutor for help.

Word count and find and replace functions are other standard features of word processing pro-

grams that can be useful to developmental writing students. The word count function helps both students and teachers keep track of the amount of development that occurs throughout the writing process. The find and replace function aids writers in using stronger verbs and avoiding repetitive word choices. So, for example, students might find variations of the *to be* verb (*is, was, were, are,* and so on), and replace those with ****; after replacing, students can reread the essay and replace the *to be* verbs with stronger choices. This strategy might lead to sentence combining and other revision techniques. Another great use is to replace *it's* with *it is* to see where *its/it's* confusion might be occurring. If a sentence becomes "The cat chased it is tail," the student will know that *its* should replace *it's*.

Saving a file properly is another important aspect of word processing. Students can use the Save As feature to save files in a format that all users can open and read. Not everyone will have the most recent version of Microsoft Word, for example. Problems may also arise between users of Macs and PCs. Have your students save to a standard file format like .rtf in order to share documents with people working from other systems. Practicing these essential communication skills will help save students from future difficulties. In addition to saving their files in the correct format, students should be careful to use consistent file naming. This practice will help both you and the students stay organized. If you are collecting twenty-five papers per class from five classes, you will want students to follow some naming conventions. One strategy for naming files is to use the student's name along with an assignment indication: for example, *MariaTrujillo_draft2_illustrationessay1*. Advise students that it is best to save work in different stages. Instead of working in one computer file as they write and revise, they should save and label different drafts as separate files. They can follow the steps below to set up a system of folders to help keep their files organized.

- Create a folder with the name of the course.

- Within the course folder, create a folder named *Writing Assignments*.

- Within the *Writing Assignments* folder, create a new folder for each assignment. Save all writing for the assignment in this folder.

- Whenever you work on a draft, use the Save As feature under the File menu to save a new version of the document with a new name: *Assign5 Tuesdraft, Assign5Weddraft, Assign5Fridraft*.

PROVIDE FEEDBACK ON STUDENT PAPERS. Instead of scribbling notes and suggestions in the side margins and a summary evaluation at the end of an essay, you can set up a computer file under the student's name, type of essay, and draft. For example, the file might be labeled *Trujillo, Maria_illustrationessay1*. As you read the essay, use a simple number key to mark the places in the essay that correspond to your suggestions, or use the comments feature in the word processing program to insert comments. To find this feature in most word processing programs, go to the Insert menu. There you will see something that says either Comment or Note. This feature will allow you to mark any spot in the essay you want to address. Your comments will then show up in the margin or as a footnote, depending on how your software is formatted. You can add summary comments at the end (perhaps in a different color font to attract attention to them), save the file, and return it to the student via e-mail.

Using a word processing program to review student essays has the following advantages.

- **NEATNESS.** The computer provides a tidy alternative to messy notes, especially after long hours of writing feedback on students' papers. Word processed comments model the orderliness and professionalism that we urge our students to use in their writing. Ironically, most instructors would not accept a paper that is written in as messy a handwriting as their feedback to students.

- **ARCHIVING.** With the computer, you can save your comments and suggestions. When reviewing subsequent drafts, it is easy to access your past comments to see how a student is progressing.

- **ADDRESSING COMMON ERRORS.** Certain errors recur in most students' papers. Examples include fragments, run-ons and comma splices, misuse of commas in compound and complex sentences, informal word choice, incorrect formatting, and so on. With the computer, you can build a file of responses to these common errors. You can also put extra effort into providing more comprehensive feedback so that each type of error is discussed with greater depth and quality. This way, you do not have to reconstruct an excellent answer multiple times for each writing weakness, sometimes repeating the same response up to twenty times per grading session over multiple grading sessions per semester.

Research

A student may now get a college degree without ever having set foot in a physical library. For faculty members who put in their time with the *Reader's Guide to Periodicals* and spent hours in the stacks as student researchers, the new reality can be hard to accept. Of course, students will benefit from learning their way around the physical library stacks, and you may wish to offer or arrange a library tutorial. But you will also want to help students learn to navigate digital research tools effectively.

Library databases that make published information searchable are good sources to which to direct students. Materials referenced in these databases were most likely selected for publication through an editorial process conducted by a newspaper, magazine, journal, or newswire service. We can explain this vetting process to students and then concentrate on helping students understand related topics: how to differentiate between magazines and journals; how to consider what type of source might be more appropriate for the type of research they are doing; how to search effectively using Boolean search methods. Many library databases come with instructions for Boolean searches. If not, those instructions and tutorials are easily found online.

The **Internet** at large also contains useful sources for your students' research papers. We might be tempted to avoid or limit our students' use of Internet sources, but we are not really doing them any favors if we do. Their lives will be inundated with questionable information. They need to learn the importance of healthy skepticism and methods for evaluating the reliability of sources.

Evaluating sources is a crucial skill in college, work, and everyday life. You might introduce your students to Internet research by sending them to mainstream or established sites that you trust. Consider using a social bookmarking tool like Delicious.com to share sources with your students or to have them share sources with one another. Source sharing through a social bookmarking site gives you an opportunity to discuss which sources you trust and why, as well as which sources appear to be more helpful and why. Teach students to ask critical questions about their sources to determine reliability. You can also direct them to *The Bedford Research Room* at **bedfordstmartins.com/researchroom/**. This comprehensive site teaches students effective online research skills and offers advice on finding, evaluating, and citing sources. Also, encourage students to check with you or a college librarian whenever they have doubts about an Internet source's reliability.

Teaching **file management** helps students to collect, store, and process information electronically. You have already addressed some file management issues if you have taught students a draft saving/naming convention for your class, how to put their own writing into folders, and how to keep their writing histories. You have taught them the elements of keeping an electronic portfolio. (For more on e-portfolios, see *Portfolio Teaching* and *Portfolio Keeping* by Nedra Reynolds and Rich Rice; ask your Bedford/St. Martin's sales rep for exam copies of these great little books.) Saving links and downloading files are much more efficient strategies while doing initial research than copying out handwritten notes or printing out articles. It saves time and paper. Students will also save time on the research process and perhaps be less likely to make documentation errors if they develop a system of typing out notes and documentation as they find information. Notetaking can be done in a word processing file or with an online tool such as Google Notebook or Evernote. Perhaps the easiest option to start with is *Bedford Bibliographer* at **bedfordstmartins.com/bibliographer/**, which is free, easy to use, includes citation creation, and offers advice from Mike Palmquist, author of *The Bedford Researcher*. If your campus supports Firefox, Zotero (www.zotero.org) is a free research tool that comes as an add-on to the Firefox browser.

You might even suggest that students use a blog as a place for research notes. With this method, students keep track of sources by linking to or citing the source in the post with notes about it. It can also help students start to think of links as a means of documenting. You will be able to talk about how and why informal ways of documenting take place online even as students are learning formal, academic documentation styles.

Online tools for online documentation are becoming increasingly common. In addition to the *Bedford Bibliographer* mentioned above, EasyBib.com and CitationMachine.net are examples of sites that help students format bibliographies. These sites require students to enter bibliographic elements into forms that then create first-draft citations. They do not automatically take information and create citations, so students still need to know what parts of a source need to be listed in a citation, where to find those elements, and in which boxes in the form to enter the information. These sites provide only first-draft citations because they are only as accurate as the information students enter. But they do help with initial formatting of the citations, and the forms serve as prompts to remind students of what information citations need, helping them to learn.

Some library databases provide bibliographic citations in MLA, APA, and other styles that students can simply cut and paste into a word processing file. These tools do not necessarily produce error-free bibliographies. The sites may not use the latest versions of the style guides or may produce bibliographies with mistakes created by students typing in incorrect information or typing in information to the wrong places. They can, however, be quite useful as students learn to format bibliographies. If nothing else, you can use these online documentation tools to create sample bibliographies to critique in class. Have students find possible corrections that are needed in the electronically generated bibliography.

E-mail

Using e-mail is a highly efficient method for instructor-student communication. Students can ask questions and you can answer them at times that are convenient to you both. Students who are reluctant to speak up in class or to visit you during your office hours may feel more comfortable asking questions through e-mail. E-mail also saves paper, which has environmental and administrative advantages: Students can e-mail their papers and assignments instead of printing them, and instructors can e-mail back their suggestions and feedback. If used effectively, e-mail can significantly cut back on paper, copying, and printing costs. As all college teachers and administrators know, these costs can be substantial.

Consider, however, that although e-mail might be more convenient for students than having to call or come by during office hours, younger students tend to consider it a formal type of communication. Text messaging, instant messaging, and online chatting are considered more informal and more immediate. (Chatting in this context refers to typing on a computer network to another person or group in real-time, and waiting for a response, then replying and sending informal messages back and forth in this manner.) It might be useful to make e-mail just one of a variety of ways students can contact you. Because e-mail is now considered the more formal choice for digital communications, discuss e-mail protocol and conventions of formal letter writing with students. One useful activity would be to work as a class on composing effective and appropriate e-mails.

Computer Projectors

Projectors and Smart Boards are now relatively common in college classrooms. If your room is equipped with projection technology, you will want to use it effectively. Educators tend to think of PowerPoint when computers and projectors are mentioned, but PowerPoint is not always the best choice.

Death by PowerPoint, the title of a 2006 book by Michael Flocker, has found its way into the education vernacular as a tongue-in-cheek description of the pervasiveness of poorly designed, boring PowerPoint lectures. Although PowerPoint can distract from the interaction between teacher and student, it does not have to. Try these three suggestions:

DO NOT USE POWERPOINT JUST TO SHARE LECTURE NOTES. This approach risks students writing instead of listening while you speak. Telling students or reading to students what they see on the PowerPoint slides and waiting for them to write it down is not effective lecturing. Many instructors like to give examples and elaborate on the information while students are writing, but the students are still, for the most part, just writing what is on the screen, and the instructor is still just walking through bullet points. With a truly vibrant, engaging lecturer, the "walking-through-bullet-points" approach might spark some great classroom interactions. In many cases, however, it deters natural classroom discussion.

PROVIDE STUDY GUIDES AND LECTURE NOTES IN WAYS THAT WILL NOT SLOW YOU DOWN IN CLASS. Ask yourself if the information in your PowerPoint slides could be distributed more efficiently through PDF files posted to a class Web site or by some other means. Make podcasts or videocasts. Post notes to blogs or to a course management system. Distributing study guides and notes using these methods frees you to use PowerPoint slides as visual stimulations and discussion prompts rather than as ways of conveying detailed information. Presentation software is not designed to share large amounts of text; use it instead to share one concept or one prompt at a time.

READ SOME BOOKS ON PRESENTATION DESIGN. Sometimes simple tweaks can make a slide much more appealing and much more effective. One excellent book on the topic is *Presentation Zen* (2008) by Garr Reynolds.

With or without PowerPoint, here are some ways you can use computer projectors or Smart Boards to facilitate classroom instruction.

- **PREWRITING.** Some prewriting activities, such as brainstorming, adapt beautifully to computer projectors. Project a prompt and have students brainstorm topics while you type them on the screen. You could also project a topic and have students brainstorm thesis statements, or project a thesis statement and have students come up with supporting points and examples.

- **THESIS STATEMENTS.** Project draft thesis statements on the screen and have students work together to improve them.

- **GRAMMAR.** Project sentences with grammar mistakes (fragments, run-ons or comma splices, punctuation errors, and so on) and have students work together to identify and correct the errors.

- **SENTENCE STYLE.** Display text with one or more of the following grammar or style problems: short, choppy sentences; wordy sentences; phrases without parallel structure; misplaced modifiers; pronouns with unclear reference; and so on. Ask students to identify and correct the errors by making appropriate revisions.

- **TECHNOLOGICAL DEMONSTRATIONS.** If students will be required to work through some technological processes on their own (Blackboard logins, accessing class wikis or blogs, using quiz sites), the projector provides an excellent way to show the students what they are supposed to do. This demonstration will mean much more to the visual learners than any written instructions they might be given.

- **GROUP ACTIVITIES.** If you use a class discussion board, blog, wiki, or any other type of online tool, you can project in class what the students have done online. Doing so can be a means of prompting discussion or helping the class as a group assess what they are accomplishing online.

Projectors and Smart Boards also help you to build up your own repository of files for classroom use. You can then share those files in multiple ways, for instance, updating students who have missed class or helping slower note takers keep up. You can also use the projectors to engage the "digital natives" in classroom activities. Students who have grown up playing video games, surfing the Internet, and enjoying the electronic gadgetry often want visual stimulation and visual clarification of information.

New Media

The explosion of new media tools in recent years has created a kind of chaos of choice. It is often difficult to know where to start changing classroom approaches and adopting new technologies. You cannot change everything at once, and you cannot use every technological tool that comes along, but you can start somewhere.

PRIVACY ISSUES. As you explore possible classroom uses for new media, keep in mind that you will also have to address the new issues created by new media. Will you require your students to engage in public writing on a blog, wiki, or social media site? Do you believe there is an ethical dilemma in requiring public writing? Can you find ways to incorporate social media while still protecting your students' privacy? You will want to discuss issues of privacy with students. Give them the option of determining how much information they want to share about themselves online, and talk to them about both the security issues involved and the kind of impression they want to make with the online presence they create.

Many social media sites allow settings to be marked private where only approved subscribers or members can view the information. If you wish to protect your students' privacy and prevent the public at large from viewing their writing, you might want to choose private settings. Either way, make informed, deliberate decisions, and be sure the students understand who has access to their writing.

Here are a few ways to incorporate new media into the classroom.

FACEBOOK/MYSPACE. Though Facebook and MySpace are often seen as distractions to schoolwork, they are effective communications tools. Students often accomplish surprising things when they are given room to be creative with social networking—and so might you. One good way to start might be to hold office hours on Facebook. Students can contact you by posting public messages on your wall, engaging in real-time chat sessions, or sending private messages to your inbox. Friending students through a designated class account gives you the opportunity to make class announcements in a space that students are more motivated to check than e-mail or Blackboard. Students could also use a social networking site as the framework for a class project. The notes or blog feature could be useful for posting portfolio items, for example. Students may also want to use the links-sharing feature for research. For class projects, you might want to insist that students create new accounts separate from the ones they use socially.

TWITTER. Microblogging sites like Twitter are great places to interact with students. The short length of the posts makes them akin to text messages, which has now become the primary means of communication for the younger generation. You can use Twitter for class announcements and class discussions. Students can choose to access the posts via cell phones or computers. Twitter can also be used to facilitate discussion in face-to-face classes. If your class Twitter stream is projected in the room as you ask questions, and your students are able to answer with their cell phones or computers, you might get interesting real-time feedback.

NING. Ning is a site that allows you to create your own social network. It is a good option for teachers who do not want to go to Facebook or MySpace. On Ning, you interact with only one network at a time as opposed to Facebook where your students might have many friends from many other contexts on the same account they are using for class. Ning will create one primary newsfeed that everyone can see. At the same time, it provides individual blogs and ways for students to share links, videos, and pictures. It can be used as a discussion forum that looks more like the type students might be accustomed to from their experiences on other social networking sites. If course management tools like Blackboard are not generating the kind of class discussion you want, consider going to Ning.

BLOGS. Blogs have many possibilities in the classroom. They can be used as class journals or as individual project management tools. A student could blog through a research project, for example. Blogs can also be used for group projects or for class discussions. They might even be used as a means for the instructor to communicate with the students by posting announcements, handouts, and instructions. Free sites like Blogger and WordPress.com offer easy ways to get started.

WIKIS. Wikis, or multi-authored Web sites, are good ways to manage group or class projects. Some classes have even created their own textbooks using wikis. If students are doing group writing assignments, consider using a wiki. Each group can create its own pages, and the collective work of the class will produce the Web site as a whole. Another use for wikis might be a class research project. If your research has a theme around which all of the students have chosen topics, the wiki might be used for sharing information found by individual students with the class. Or maybe you want to make a grammar wiki with students themselves creating lessons and examples. Once you familiarize yourself with a wiki platform like Wet Paint, PB Wiki, or Google Sites, you will find any number of uses for it.

THE GOOGLE SUITE. With a free gmail account, you gain access to a whole suite of Google products. With Google Sites, you can make an individual or a group Web site. With Google Docs you can make individual or collaborative word processing, presentation, or spreadsheet files that can be shared selectively or published to the Web. With Google Groups, you can create e-mail lists or discussion forums. Blogger is also included in a gmail account. Other products by other companies accomplish many of these same things, but Google docs offer free accounts and collaborative features that make their products very useful for the classroom.

SOCIAL BOOKMARKING. Delicious, Citeulike, Blackboard Scholar, and Zotero are examples of social bookmarking tools. These sites allow you to gather and share links to useful resources. They also allow for tagging or labeling bookmarks by topics. These are useful ways for teachers to share links with students, for students to share with each other, and for teachers to track student progress on research.

AUDIOCASTING. If you communicate online with your students at all, you might want to consider making audio recordings to share; after all, the spoken word is one of our most powerful means of teaching. You need only a computer and a microphone to get started. Download a free audio recording program like Audacity to produce mp3 files or check with your school's tech support to find out

if it subscribes to Wimba or other podcasting software for Blackboard. You can also do a search for a Web site that will allow you to make online recordings. AudioBoo, for example, allows iPhone users to simply call in audio recordings. No computer or microphone is required.

In addition to creating your own audio recordings, you can find and share helpful audio programs. Mignon Fogarty's *Grammar Girl* podcast is one of the most popular shows on iTunes, and it is free. Your students might truly benefit from it or other educational podcasts. (See the *Student Center for Real Skills* at bedfordstmartins.com/realskills for links to relevant *Grammar Girl* podcasts.) And because students can download podcasts to listen to while they are doing other things, this form of education complements the mobile, multitasking lifestyles of many students today.

VIDEOCASTING. Like audiocasting, videocasting is increasingly common and increasingly useful in education. Many digital cameras now come with video capabilities, and laptops often come with built-in Web cams. Simple digital video cameras have also become much more affordable. Additionally, screencasting software for creating video tutorials now comes in free versions like Jing. Videocasting is a good option for both online and face-to-face teachers. Try posting videos to YouTube or TeacherTube, or create video lectures on a site like Seesmic using your Web cam. Also like audiocasting, plenty of educational videos are available online. You do not always have to create your own. Search YouTube or other social video sites for clips that will be useful to your students.

E-portfolios

E-portfolios, or electronic portfolios, are more and more important to the writing classroom. They can be assigned as project portfolios, class portfolios, or career portfolios. In any of these variations, they offer a chance to write with and through technology that is essential to basic literacy in the digital age.

Some schools purchase e-portfolio platforms that provide ways to grade, record, and track student progress in addition to the tools for creating portfolios. Others adopt e-portfolio building blocks for Blackboard or other course management systems. If your school has access to one of these options, consider using it. If not, there are plenty of free options.

VISUALCV.COM. VisualCV is a free site that allows for online CV building. It also provides space for uploading text files and linking out to other sites, making it a perfect place to build a career portfolio.

WIKIS. Wet Paint, PB Wiki, and other wiki sites could be used for project, class, or career portfolios. Because wikis are designed for collaborative work, they are great for group projects and portfolios. They do not have to be used collaboratively, however. They could easily be adapted to create a student's career portfolio or Web site.

BLOGS. Blogger and WordPress are just two of the many free blogging sites available. Blogs are an interesting way to create portfolios. One approach might be to publish the portfolio items in blog posts, saving the last post (the one that will show up at the top) for the portfolio introduction. Another method is to link to portfolio items in the side bar and have only one post that serves as an introduction. If this approach is used, consider publishing portfolio artifacts as Google Docs. This approach provides an easy, free way to link to text files.

GOOGLE DOCS + PRESENTATION. Presentation slides can be used as introductions to individual portfolio artifacts. Publishing items in Google Docs that then link to Google Presentation works well. This also invites the opportunity to work with presentation design as part of the project. Another advantage is that Google Presentations can be either published to the Web or shared with select viewers. The latter option might be an answer for students reluctant to make their writing public.

Regardless of which e-portfolio option you choose, from those discussed above or another, you will help students create something they can be proud of when you assign an e-portfolio. You will also help them learn some of the basic delivery methods of twenty-first-century literacy. (For more on using writing portfolios, see Chapter 11 in this manual.)

Addressing Plagiarism

Preventing plagiarism is hard work. Fears that cheating is more common in the digital age may be well founded. It is as tempting for instructors to turn to electronic plagiarism detection services

such as Turnitin.com or SafeAssign, a plagiarism detection option that comes free with Blackboard 6.0 or higher, as it is for students to copy and paste writing assignments from online sources. There is no single answer to preventing plagiarism, however. Do not consider plagiarism detection services the primary way to address the issue.

The biggest deterrents to plagiarism are student engagement in the assignment and instructor involvement in the student writing process. Students might cheat for a variety of reasons: They care about the grade but not the assignment; they feel overwhelmed and underconfident; their attention has been on other things; cheating is easy enough to be tempting. We might not be able to guess exactly why a student has cheated, but we do know he or she is less likely to cheat (1) if the assignment itself matters to the student as much as the grade, (2) if cheating is more trouble than doing the assignment, and (3) if the assignment is stepped out in drafts and evolves from class discussions or freewriting or brainstorming that you assign. We also know that not all plagiarism is deliberate cheating. For more on addressing plagiarism, including additional handouts you can use in your course, visit **bedfordstmartins.com/plagiarism** for *The Bedford/St. Martin's Workshop on Plagiarism.*

Before deciding whether or not to use a plagiarism detection service, consider other ways to prevent plagiarism.

- **MAKE SURE STUDENTS UNDERSTAND PLAGIARISM AND YOUR POLICIES REGARDING PLAGIARISM.** Remember that some skills, like proper paraphrasing and documentation, are difficult to master even after they have been covered in class. In fact, these skills are difficult even for upper-level students and professionals; they will certainly be difficult for the new and struggling college student. Assume that initial mistakes in documentation, even to the extent of copying too much text from sources, are opportunities to learn rather than deliberate acts of academic dishonesty.

- **GIVE UNIQUE ASSIGNMENTS THAT APPLY TO STUDENTS' LIVES.** Using the same topics as other instructors or the same topics from semester to semester invites students to recycle past papers. A plagiarism detection service will detect this kind of cheating only if students upload the shared essays to the same database. Make it more difficult from the start for students to borrow from friends or from Web sites by changing your assignments often.

- **SPEND TIME RESPONDING TO EARLY DRAFTS.** Consider assigning portfolios that require multiple drafts with significant revision. This technique will make you more aware of your students' writing styles and make it more difficult for them to find papers to copy.

- **WALK YOUR STUDENTS THROUGH THE WHOLE PROCESS OF WRITING.** Talk to them about their writing even in prewriting stages. Get to know their ideas and their thinking on the subject. Find out if they are feeling overwhelmed or if they need extra help coming up with ideas. Challenge them to move beyond vague, general ideas that might leave room later for copying from others.

All these strategies for avoiding plagiarism are practices of good writing instruction whether technological tools are involved or not. No tool is a substitute for what the teacher does.

Let us now discuss some of the issues related to using plagiarism detection services. These tools have been as controversial as they are popular. If your school or department has adopted Turnitin or another service, you may or may not decide to use it with your students, but you should first make sure you are aware of the controversy.

Many complaints have been made against Turnitin and services like it, but those complaints mainly fall into three main categories: (1) problematizing instructor–student relations, (2) infringing on the students' intellectual property rights, and (3) questionable reliability.

INSTRUCTOR–STUDENT RELATIONS. Use of a plagiarism detection service could send the message that the instructor assumes the students are cheating, which is not a healthy attitude for good working relations. In addition, there is the risk that the tool might be used for punitive measures rather than instructional measures. If the plagiarism detection service is used only to catch students doing something wrong, then we do have to question what instructional value it really has and whether its value is worth the potentially damaged trust between instructor and student.

INTELLECTUAL PROPERTY RIGHTS. When your students upload writing to Turnitin, their work goes into a database where it is compared with other items in the Turnitin databases. Turnitin then keeps your students' writing in its databases to compare other essays to it in the future. A school can find out if students are sharing essays by building up its own repository in a plagiarism detection service database. This presents an ethical issue, however, in that Turnitin then profits from its large database of student writing while the students themselves receive no compensation. In addition, the students do not voluntarily submit their work to the database; they are compelled to do so in class. Because of this use of students' intellectual property, some instructors avoid using Turnitin.

RELIABILITY. A plagiarism detection service is simply an electronic tool. It runs on a formula like spell checkers. It does not have human intuition or reasoning skills. It is accurate no more often than a grammar checking program. It does what it is designed to do, but it is not perfect. The question for the instructor then is whether the reliability level is worth the cost, since students usually pay for the use of this service. The instructor should always question whether the student is getting his or her money's worth.

If you decide not to use Turnitin or SafeAssign, you can also try free online sites such as www.articlechecker.com and www.plagiarismchecker.com. These sites are useful for quick checks of suspicious materials. Whole passages can be copied in. The programs then run searches for Web matches. These programs search only the Web; they have no databases of their own and cannot check subscription library databases. They will work, however, to locate blatant cases of Internet copying and pasting. A simple Google search on a suspicious title, phrase, or sentence can also often yield faster and more accurate results than paid services.

If you do decide to use Turnitin or another plagiarism detection service, think about ways you can use it as an instructional tool rather than a punitive one. Remember that the percentage identified as unoriginal in the reports does not necessarily mean that exact percentage is plagiarized. It is also possible that none of the writing is plagiarized. For example, Turnitin might mark something like "In our society today, we often think . . ." as unoriginal. It is indeed unoriginal, but it is not plagiarism. Also, Turnitin.com and SafeAssign both support calling an assignment a draft, which lets you and students run a check to see if there is matching text. After the check, students can revise the draft to address any matching text that is not properly cited.

Practice some of these techniques to avoid the issue of compromised student–instructor relations when using a plagiarism detection service:

- Make sure students understand what the plagiarism detection service is and what it does before assignments are uploaded.

- Make sure students are aware of your plagiarism policy before assignments are uploaded.

- Give students full access to their own originality reports.

- Allow students to upload rough drafts to the plagiarism detection service so that they have a chance to make corrections if unintentional plagiarism is found.

- Go over a sample originality report with students (perhaps on a piece of your own writing) so that you can talk about which items marked would be considered plagiarism, which would be correctly documented quotations, and which would be simply unoriginal language that is not actual plagiarism.

- Use instances of unoriginality in writing as opportunities to learn how to be more original. Do not use the reports simply to find and punish wrongdoing.

- Understand that the number given as the percent plagiarized in the report means little, given that some of the items marked might be acts of deliberate plagiarism, some might be acts of unintentional plagiarism, and some might not be plagiarism at all.

- Do not expect the originality reports to be infallible. Just as they will sometimes mark sentences that are clichéd but not plagiarized, they will also sometimes miss passages that are plagiarized. Ultimately, you should work from your own judgment just as you would without the plagiarism detection service.

Using Course Management Tools

COURSE MANAGEMENT SYSTEMS (CMS). Using programs like Blackboard, WebCT, or Moodle, you can develop custom Web sites tailored to your courses' individual needs. Check your college's Web site or ask your IT department which system might be available to you. You can also use Bedford/St. Martin's online course space *WritingClass*. Loaded with instructional material, engaging activities, and simple writing tools, *WritingClass* helps students keep up with their assignments and lets them work whenever they have time, wherever they have Web access. (For more information on *WritingClass*, see the section on Using the Ancillary Package in Chapter 1 of this manual.) Many schools now require instructors to use CMS, so becoming familiar with these tools is important. Here is some basic information to get you started.

WHAT COURSE MANAGEMENT TOOLS ARE. Course management tools allow you to post syllabi announcements, assignments, and other course materials to a Web site that your students can access. They might also provide communication tools such as chat rooms and discussion boards. These tools can be used as an aid to traditional face-to-face classes, or they may be a key part of distance-learning courses.

HOW TO GET STARTED. If your school requires you to use a CMS, chances are good that the school also provides training. Take advantage of any training that is available.

Your school's technology staff should be able to set you up with an account, a password, and a basic shell for your course content and answer whatever questions you have. Your CMS may come with training or support tools that you can access whenever you need help. Search the company site for the CMS platform provider for possible video tutorials. You will also often find free tutorials on YouTube.

If you are using a CMS for the first time, leave yourself plenty of time before the first class to become familiar with the system. Understand what types of information you can post and decide what content makes the most sense for your class. Also, take time before the first class to post sample content and check links. You might want to work with another instructor who is teaching the same course or a similar course to test each other's content and determine best practices.

HOW TO BUILD YOUR SITE. Major CMSs such as Blackboard and WebCT include features like course information, course documents, external links, and discussion boards. In the course information area, you might want to include such items as your course syllabus and schedule, the school's plagiarism policy, and any other documents that spell out general policies and procedures.

You might use the course documents section to post handouts on course content, additional readings, and other materials. You can include assignments here, perhaps posting them and removing them as needed so that students are not overwhelmed or confused. You can organize course documents by week or topic, whatever works best for you.

In the external links section, you can provide links to all kinds of online writing help, including the *Student Center for Real Skills* at bedfordstmartins.com/realskills or *Re:Writing,* a collection of writing resources at bedfordstmartins.com/rewriting. You might also include a link to your school library's Web site or to sites recommended by librarians or colleagues.

Discussion boards allow you to set up discussions on concepts, assignments, or readings that you are covering in class. Or you might post open-ended questions or prompts for response. Many instructors find that students who freeze up when told they must write a paper write freely in online discussion forums; in fact, they may do some of their best writing on discussion boards and truly become engaged in communicating with their peers. For this reason, online discussion can serve as prewriting for longer, more polished papers.

Decide how involved you want to be in online discussions. Some instructors add to or comment on their students' discussions frequently, while others stay out of the conversation for the most part, maintaining the discussion board as a "student space." Whatever level of involvement you choose, explain the ground rules for online discussion early in the semester. For instance, encourage students to stay on topic whenever possible, and explain that profanity and personal attacks will not be tolerated.

Another good approach early in the semester is to ask students to introduce themselves in a brief posting. They can write about their children or families, their reasons for going to college, their current jobs or the jobs they want to get, or their interests outside of work and school. Students might then comment on each other's postings.

Be aware that special course management content is available with *Real Skills*. This content includes online tests and quizzes and online discussion prompts.

For First Timers

If you are teaching in a computer classroom for the first time, the following advice should help you feel more in control.

- Arrive early. It takes time to turn computers on and check peripherals.

- If you have a networked area, do not position yourself in front of your computer and not budge. Developmental students need one-on-one reinforcement from their instructor. Move around the room.

- Do not always teach from one position. Move from board to overhead to student stations. Your moving allows all students the opportunity to hear you clearly above the hum of the computers.

- When you lecture and give instructions to be followed later, have students darken their screens so they will listen to you. Otherwise, they may pay more attention to the computer than to you.

- Help students out by providing detailed handouts on assignments. Include specifics on what you want: type of writing, acceptable topics, due dates for drafts, peer editing, final copy, and materials to be submitted with final drafts.

- Be patient with students who may need special orientation and reminders on using the computers. If your computer and software has a built-in tutorial, use it with your students. Students can progress at their own speed without feeling either rushed or held back. You may want to prepare a worksheet for students to complete as they work through a tutorial. Whether using a prepared tutorial or walking students through an introduction, devote at least one class session to learning how to use the computers before you give a writing assignment.

- Go slowly. Blend writing and computer instruction. Introduce just a little bit of information at a time. Make sure students are comfortable with basic word processing before introducing any editing features.

- When introducing a new task on the computer, keep the class together. Be sure each student is with you. Do not let students work ahead. Have those students who finish early help their classmates.

- Prepare simple handouts that students can take with them to the labs detailing all of the tasks they will need to perform with the various software programs. Even if the computer or software manuals are available, few people want to read them. If they are frustrating to you, imagine how the developmental student would feel trying to make sense out of one.

Possible Problems and Solutions

When incorporating computers into the developmental curriculum, expect the unexpected and remain flexible. However, because you want to be as prepared as possible, here are a few situations that could occur and some ideas for handling them.

COMPUTER-PHOBIC STUDENTS. Though we now expect students to have some prior experience with computers, they do not always come to our classes feeling comfortable about their computer skills. Some, especially older or returning students, may have had very little exposure to computers. For those students, keep up the encouragement by assuring them they will enjoy writing with the computer. In addition, be extremely patient with their endless questions. Do not show exasperation when they seem to forget instructions from one day to the next. Usually, the light will dawn, and they will finally grasp what to do and when to do it. Refrain from doing any task yourself that you want students to learn how to do. If a student asks how to save or quit for the day, for example, you can stand behind the student and verbally walk him or her through the process. But keep your hands off the mouse or keyboard. The student will learn only from first-hand experience.

COMPUTERPHILIC STUDENTS. On the opposite end of the spectrum are the students who are computer whizzes (or at least think they are). These students create a different set of problems because they do not want to wait for instructions. In addition, they get frustrated with their slower classmates, or they cause disruptions because they finish an assignment early and want to play around or visit with other classmates (even if those classmates have not finished). You can relieve some of these problems by asking at the beginning of the semester who has experience with computers, especially the kind that you are using in class. Then ask those students to be your assistants. You can explain that alone, you cannot quickly get to all students with computer or printer problems, so you could use their help. Also, when you introduce a new program or a new assignment, ask everyone to stay with you. Point out that the computer-savvy students may understand the computer, but they do not know exactly what you want. Again, you might privately ask a stronger computer user to keep an alert eye toward a student who sits close by who appears to have problems following your directions.

Note that some computerphilic students will use the computer to surf the Internet, send e-mail or text messages to friends, check their MySpace or Facebook pages, or play games during class. As with cell-phone use, during the first class you should state your policy regarding non-class-related computer activities. If you do not want students on Facebook during class, make your policy clear.

DIFFICULTY ADJUSTING TO WRITING ON A COMPUTER. Even a computer-literate student may have a bad writing day and sit staring at the screen. These situations are easily handled when you move around the room as your students are working. If you notice a student just sitting, stop and chat. Try to determine what the problem is. Sometimes, students merely zone out for a few moments because they are tired, thinking about a test in another class, or merely trying to figure out what to say next. If the student is struggling for the right words during the writing of a first draft, offer suggestions on how to continue: typing the first word that comes to mind or entering a string of question marks to indicate a word problem, for example. Remind the student that the draft is not a final version. He or she will have plenty of time to revise and find the perfect word. If the student has not done the assigned preparation, recommend starting at that point and suggest that he or she visit the lab after class to catch up. You can also take the time to talk through the writing with the student. Often, students know what they want to write, but they cannot think of a way to write it. If you have them tell you orally, you can then say, "Okay, type what you just told me." Or you can suggest that the student just start typing—freewriting to see where the subject will go.

If students do not ask you for help, ask yourself why. Have you isolated yourself from the students by staying at your own computer? If so, walk around and perhaps read over a few shoulders. By making yourself more accessible, you will perhaps make students more comfortable about asking for assistance. Also, remember that some students do not need help. They are self-motivated and have done their homework, so when they get to class they are ready to begin writing and want to be left alone. Those students will usually come to you when they hit a rough spot. In addition, some students prefer to ask another student rather than the teacher. (Remember when one student helps another, both can benefit.) However, some students have been rejected by teachers in the past or may feel intimidated by a teacher. Your friendliness and frequent offers of assistance may eventually turn some of those students around, but others may never feel comfortable asking for help.

MECHANICAL PROBLEMS. Mechanical problems may be harder to deal with. You will be more comfortable in the classroom and save a tremendous amount of time if you learn everything you can about the computers. Work with your college's support staff to find out the typical problems that you might face (or read the computer manual's troubleshooting guide). Then, ask for guidance on quickly correcting the problem. Some problems with nonworking computers or printers are relatively simple to solve:

- Check the power switch.

- Check cable connections.

- Make sure the student is using the correct printer.

Sometimes computers overload and freeze up, which is a frustrating problem. You can often get a frozen computer working again simply by restarting it. Here is the safest way to reboot a PC: While pressing down the *Ctrl* and *Alt* keys, press the *Delete* key. This keystroke combination will usually allow you to close any programs that are running but not responding. Closing programs before rebooting will help prevent system problems. It is amazing how often this relatively simple solution does the job.

Unfortunately, not all problems are simple. A computer crash can fall into that category. If the crash was caused by a power surge or momentary power outage, then the computer will start working as soon as the power comes back on. However, anything that the students have done since they last saved will be lost. Therefore, remind students often to save their documents every few minutes. Tell them that the few seconds the process requires can save them the frustration of reconstructing an hour's worth of work after a power outage.

If a classroom has a problem that you cannot fix, request help from your school's computer support staff. (Familiarize yourself with the procedure for requesting assistance so you will know what to do if the occasion arises.) Since some problems will not be fixed during class, always have a backup plan so that you can comfortably continue teaching without the computer.

8

Using Learning Styles and Other Instructional Approaches

(with learning-styles advice from Connie Gulick, TVI Community College, Albuquerque)

Every instructor makes use of a different set of pedagogical tools—and we can all benefit from learning about the tools that other people use. This chapter is a compendium of classroom techniques that other instructors and I have used over the years and have found to be helpful to our students. Some topics that you might expect to see covered here (e.g., collaboration, critical thinking, and bringing the real world into the classroom) are treated in depth in other chapters of this manual. This chapter is a grab bag, with brief suggestions for a wide variety of approaches, all of which are supported by the pedagogy and resources of *Real Skills*. I hope you find at least a couple of ideas that you want to try out in your next semester.

Use Learning Styles

Your class will probably consist of students who have a variety of learning styles: visual, verbal, auditory, hands-on, and interpersonal, as well as linear. There are a variety of methods of classifying learning styles, but the exact details of the scheme matter less than recognizing that the students in your class are tuned to a variety of different frequencies. If you broadcast your message on a single frequency (with linear, abstract lectures), you will connect with some people but miss others. Varying the pedagogy is a way to reach more students. Students typically learn well, enjoy the class,

and pay close attention when you vary the classroom activities.

A varied pedagogy can also help by breaking things up—it is difficult for anyone to concentrate on a single voice talking in a single format for forty-five minutes, and it is especially difficult for students with attention deficit/hyperactivity disorder (ADHD) or other learning disabilities. (See Chapter 3, Working with Developmental Writers, for an overview of teaching students with ADHD or other learning disabilities.) Almost anything that departs from the normal pace or format can be useful: Small-group instruction, group work, one-on-one conferences, student presentations, independent study, and discussions are just a few of the possibilities.

Real Skills makes it easy to address a variety of learning preferences in your classroom. Early in the semester, ask students to take the learning-styles inventory in Chapter 3. Students can also take the test online at www.vark-learn.com. This helps students determine whether they are visual, auditory, reading/writing (verbal), or kinesthetic (movement) learners, or some combination of these types. The part of the chapter titled "Use Your Learning Style in College" suggests activities—in *Real Skills* and beyond—that can help students become better readers and writers by making use of their learning styles. If you want to emphasize learning styles, you might take some time to go over this chapter in class and emphasize that symbols in *Real Skills* indicate activities geared to certain learning preferences.

Because students in your class will have many different learning preferences, it will not be possible to individualize instruction to each student, nor is that ideal. All students can benefit from varied instruction, and most will find it enjoyable. A fun way to engage all kinds of students is to assign some of the Practice Together activities at the end of most chapters in *Real Skills*. These activities help students improve their writing and editing skills while collaborating with peers.

Here are a few guidelines for planning lessons that address a variety of learning styles.

- Think, *How can I show this concept in a different way from what I was taught?* For example, if you learned a grammar rule through reading it, make up a song about the rule, or illustrate the rule. Then, show the concept using both the traditional and your new way. When explaining difficult concepts especially, using more than one teaching method is helpful.

- Make your students move to stretch their legs and get their blood to pumping. Have students post their writing or other work on the walls and then wander around to read others' work. (The Practice Together sections in *Real Skills* include several activities of this type.)

- When you discuss something new, like subject-verb agreement, talk it through first, working through the thought process. (For example, *Ben ____ the guitar. Ben is what kind of subject? Singular. So it needs what kind of verb? Singular. Singular verbs end in* s *in the present tense.* Ben plays *the guitar.*) Write down examples as you talk through them to reinforce the concepts.

- Draw pictures, as well as write, on the board. It does not matter if you are not an artist. Students will appreciate the attempt even if all you manage is stick figures. We English teachers like to use analogies. Just turn those analogies into pictures.

- All students can improve on their least preferred styles by practicing them along with their most preferred styles. Again, you will not be able to individualize instruction to learning styles, much less keep track of all the preferences in your class. However, after students take the learning-styles inventory in Chapter 3 of *Real Skills*, suggest that they make a note of their least preferred style and that they try to "exercise" it whenever possible. Trying a variety of learning methods will help lessons "stick."

Encourage Active Learning

A Chinese philosopher once said, "What I hear, I forget. What I see, I remember. What I do, I understand." This quotation provides an excellent motto for teaching. Experience shows that students learn best via active and interactive processing over time. As the Learning Pyramid on page 94 illustrates, the more actively involved people become with their own learning, the more they will retain. With active learning, students make the course content their own—both by processing it in a way that makes sense to them and by investing their own energy in it. The students take charge of the learning; we merely facilitate. Or as one of my colleagues says, "In active learning, the teacher is the band master who directs but never plays an instrument during the performance."

Active learning does not mean that instructors relinquish control of the class to students. If anything, it requires a great deal of preparation to create the best possible context—and then the fortitude to sit back while students forge their own way within that context. For active learning to work, tasks must

- Have built-in motivators.
- Be relevant to students' needs and goals.
- Be do-able.
- Be satisfying.

Much of the pedagogy of *Real Skills* is based on the model of active learning. The entire real-world component assumes that succeeding in the worlds of college, work, and everyday life is a primary motivating factor for students—students will be motivated to tackle writing tasks if they can see the immediate relevance and applicability to these arenas. The instructional focus is on whole-paragraph and whole-essay assignments, rather than unconnected drills, so that writing tasks are satisfying and create a sense of closure and accomplishment. The grammar chapters typically begin with an Understand section; then students move on to a Find and Correct section to work on common grammar errors, and an Edit section in which they can learn how to self-edit. In other words, students move from being passive recipients of knowledge to active participants who apply skills to tasks that mean something to them, from the top of the Learning Pyramid to the base.

Active learning can happen within many contexts, including individual work, small-group work, one-on-one conferences, large-group work, reading, writing, talking, listening, and reflecting. Journal writing, peer evaluations, and collaboration are forms of active learning that we use frequently (these are discussed in detail in other sections of this manual). Here are some additional suggestions:

- Ask specific prediscussion questions, and let your students know that you will call on anyone in the class. In class, build on their homework. Discuss and use the questions in either small or large groups.

- Place a suggestion box in the room and encourage students to make written comments every time the class meets. Give them a few minutes during class to do so.

- Before a test, pair students so that they can quiz each other or write sample sentences illustrating a particular rule of grammar or punctuation.

- Encourage study partners—this format not only helps students interact but also places more of the responsibility for learning on their shoulders.

- Ask students to paraphrase in two or three sentences, either orally or in their journals, what you have discussed during that day's class.

- Assign a quick-response paper (sometimes referred to as a one-minute paper). Ask the class to answer two questions in one sentence each: (1) What was the most useful/meaningful thing you learned during this session? (2) What question(s) remains uppermost in your mind as we end this session?

- Use the RSQC2 technique, in which students **R**ecall the most interesting or significant points of the previous class, **S**ummarize important points in one sentence, raise any **Q**uestions that they still have about the topic, **C**omment in a word or phrase on how they felt about the discussion during that class, and **C**onnect what they learned during the last class with previous classes or with the next assignment.

- Encourage students to become active readers: Have them read, discuss, and practice the suggestions for active, critical reading in Chapter 2 of *Real Skills*. You might also have them work through the close-reading questions in the margins of the essays at the end of the book.

- Use the ideas for self-assessment included in Chapter 10 of this manual. Placing students in the role of evaluator helps them to see the big picture and take responsibility for their own progress.

To encourage active learning, you may need to reevaluate your approach to certain activities or assignments. Too often, our typical behavior reflects and maintains a notion of learners as passive recipients rather than active participants. Give students the time and space to be active.

- Allow sufficient wait time when you ask a question. Too often, we answer the questions ourselves before students really have a chance.

- Move around the room as students are writing, and answer questions that come up as they work.

- Encourage students to ask a question whenever they have one. Remind them that the best time to ask a question is when they think of it. Instead of giving pat answers, probe student comments and ask follow-up questions.

- Offer students the chance to voice their opinions about what you are doing in class, the topics you have assigned, the homework, or even the course itself.

- Remember that when you place students in groups for the first time, they may be shy and uncomfortable. (You may want to consider cultural tensions as well. Muslim women, for example, may feel uncomfortable in a group with men.) Therefore, allow some get-acquainted time and try not to move the discussion along too rapidly. Suggest that students introduce themselves to each other and that they briefly discuss what they hope to get out of the day's activity.

Active-learning techniques serve many purposes. Aside from the most important aspect of making the student more accountable for his or her learning, they can also relieve some stress for the teacher. Increased participation can lead to more interesting classes and less need for lectures. Active-learning techniques can also help your students interact with each other and with you. Some activities can help you and your students get to know each other or break the ice. In addition, some activities give you an opportunity to assess understanding without the actual grading. Active learning can help students relate to the subject and can help everyone get the fullest possible benefit from the class.

Getting Students to Do the Readings
Linda B. Nilson, *Clemson University*

Why Students Skip the Readings

Students have a lot going on these days: part-time and even full-time jobs, "real lives" with family and household responsibilities, homework for multiple courses, community service commitments, and physical fitness routines—not to mention less noble activities like parties, football games, hobbies, "obligatory" television programs, Internet entertainment, and other forms of fun. Who has time for reading assignments?

Besides, as students reason, not doing the readings has no consequences. The next test is weeks away, and what good will the readings do anyway? They did not do them in high school and still got good enough grades to get this far. Certainly, skipping the readings in college will not hurt their chances of landing that lucrative first they aspire to and expect. Bottom line: The professor will lecture the *Reader's Digest* version of the chapters during the next class anyway.

With little practice in "book learning," it is not surprising that few students are proficient in reading academic material. Most read passively, superficially, and rather slowly, averaging 100–250 words per minute, depending on the technical density of the text.

At this speed, reading fifty 500-word pages would take students from 100 minutes to over four hours. Of course, these estimates assume that they can focus their attention on the text for so long. But many cannot focus for even five minutes, so they give up after a few pages.

What can faculty do to help students and push them to finish their reading?

It may seem too obvious to mention, but the first thing you must do if you want your students to do the readings for your class is to get your students to buy the required books. At the first class meeting, tell them that they will have to read and possibly even mark up the books daily for a chance at a passing final grade. If they cannot or will not buy the books, they should drop your course.

Be realistic in selecting the books, articles, Web pages, and other materials that you assign. Do not choose a reading because you like it. As an expert in the field, you have internalized all the cognitive shortcuts that make it easy reading for you. Consider that your average student's reading ability is probably marginal at best, and his or her love of sophisticated nonfiction less than passionate. Look for readings with graphics and pictures that reinforce the text and pare down the required pages to the essentials. The less reading assigned the more likely students will do it. If you are uncertain about the reading level of an assignment, get a quick analysis at www.harrymclaughlin.com/SMOG.htm.

SELL STUDENTS ON THE READINGS
Everyone else is trying to sell our students something. Why aren't we? Do not assume that your students think you have their best interests at heart.

Explain why you chose the readings you did, as well as their purpose, value, and relevance to the course. Students see this as a sign of respect. Make explicit connections between the readings and in-class activities, written assignments, and exams. Preview and promote the next reading assignment in class, and help students over the hump by letting them start reading key pieces in class. Finally, stop lecturing the readings in class. Extend or update the material in the readings, or clarify what you know students will not grasp on their own. But you cannot expect rational people to do the reading if the knowledge will be spoon-fed to them in class the next day.

TEACH READING STRATEGIES

Chances are your students are not familiar with how textbooks and academic publications are structured, so take a little class time for them to peruse the table of contents, the introduction, and the chapter/section layout. Have them identify "road signs" like headings, subheadings, and bold and italicized text. Why send them into foreign territory without a map?

Teach students how an expert reads, and it is not from the first word to the last. In order to anticipate the content of a particular reading, we often preview it, skimming through the subheadings, graphics, and italicized words on our way to the conclusion, which we typically read first. Thus, we start at the beginning of a piece already knowing its destination and a bit about how it gets there. Why not share this cognitively efficient reading strategy with our students?

Further, expert readers read with a purpose. As a rule, we are looking for something that is useful and important to our work. Students often tackle assigned readings with no purpose at all, so we have to give them one: study questions to answer, for example, or problems to solve (end-of-chapter or our own).

This type of assignment cues students as to what we consider important, something they desperately want to know. We should have them write out and turn in their answers or solutions and give them points for a good-faith effort. Additionally, we should have them write out or concept-map a summary of the readings.

Another expert reading method to teach your students is marginalia, which is actually teaching them how to recognize "the main point" of a passage.

Lead an in-class exercise on a few pages of an assigned reading in which the students write three to five words next to each paragraph either summa-rizing or reacting to the material (your choice). Also have them underline a few key words and phrases—no more than 10 percent of the text. Then have them justify their marginalia and underlining choices and compare their choices against yours.

In a similiar way, you can teach your students a related reading strategy: highlighting with discernment. In Weimer's (2005) two-class technique, she builds highlighting into the first two reading assignments and moderates two class discussions about what her students highlighted versus what she highlighted. In this way, students learn what an expert's reasons are for distinguishing some text as central and other text as support or elaboration.

HOLD STUDENTS ACCOUNTABLE FOR THE READINGS

If we do not grade students on an assignment, they think we regard it as unimportant. So to communicate to students the value of the readings, we have to assign reading-related activities that are worth points—enough throughout the semester to total at least 20 percent of the final grade.

Since you are grading on a good-faith effort, you need not commit or correct. Just allocate points for students' meeting the reasonable length requirement you set and demonstrating familiarity with the readings. You can grade these activities as complexly as a 3/2/1/0 points system or as simply 1/0. Best of all, grading these efforts not only motivates students to read but also enhances their learning and retention.

One accountability option is written homework, like having students respond in writing to the study questions or problems mentioned above. Students now average only three hours of homework per week for each course, so it is not unreasonable to expect that they can do more. Further, you can extend the homework into in-class activities.

Another effective alternative is the daily quiz on the readings' major points. For online, pre-class administration, many faculty rely on electronic test banks for basic-level multiple-choice items, which essentially grade themselves. If you print out items for an in-class quiz, you can first have students take it individually and turn it in, then have small groups retake it as a unit. This second step allows for students to talk about the readings. For higher-level quizzing that requires thinking beyond recall, you can compose an in-class mini-essay question. To save time, you can dictate it or display it on a slide. Judging a good-faith effort will take you only seconds.

Once you stop lecturing the readings, you will have abundant class time for the third possible activity—in-class written exercises that have students restate, apply, summarize, examine, and/or assess the readings. For instance, students can work on problem solutions to turn in or to present to the class, or they can do any number of writing-to-learn exercises, such as freewriting on the main points in the readings. The key is to make most or all of the task an individual one, so that a nonreader cannot hide behind a reader, then to grade the product on a good-faith effort.

Finally, you can hold your class accountable with some kind of in-class oral activity on the readings, preferably where you cold-call on students and, again, grade their answer on a good-faith effort. You can start with recitation (recall) questions and move into throught-inducing discussion questions, or even simulations and role plays that require the knowledge in the readings. To ensure "random" cold-calling, put each of your students' names on an index card and shuffle the deck. Mark the good-faith "grade" on the card, return the card to the deck, and shuffle again. Do not let anyone feel too safe or get too comfortable!

Students Will Do the Readings

After attending one of my workshops, Clemson University English instructor Skye Suttie instituted daily quizzes in her classes. Each day she had her students write an answer to a general, open-ended question on the readings. She found "they worked like a charm! . . . I noticed a huge change in the grade as the semester progressed. They were actually sometimes disappointed on days when I opted not to give them quizzes!"

Mick Lalopa, associate professor of Hospitality and Tourism Management at Purdue University, witnessed a similar transformation in his students. For years most of them had not been doing the readings and, as a result, were gleaning little from his PowerPoint-studded lectures. Then, after perusing the literature on increasing reading compliance, he started requiring his students to write "detailed study notes" on the assigned readings, which they turned in for a grade.

"The technique has worked wonders," Lalopa claims. He opens the discussion with the broad question "What did you learn about _____ in chapter _____?" With this and a few follow-up questions, most of the class participates in articulating the key points. "Best of all," he continues, "the students indicated that they were HAPPY that they were being required to prepare study notes because it forced them to read the chapter."

Use Journals

To encourage students to write abundantly and freely, consider journal writing as a requirement in your course. Journals provide practice in thinking on paper, and journal entries can later be revised and refined for a formal writing assignment. They also encourage self-growth and exploration and give you some insight into your students' lives and thoughts.

I find three entries per week (one-half to one page each) a reasonable requirement. Ask students to number and/or date each entry, and encourage them to set aside certain times each week to write. Some students enjoy arriving in class early, taking out their journals and writing for ten minutes before class begins. To strongly emphasize the importance of regular writing, you can set aside five to ten minutes of every class to have students write in their journals. If you are in a computer classroom, you might want to try an online journal. (See Chapter 7 of this manual for more on online journals.)

Suggest that students either write their journal entries on regular notebook paper or type them into the computer and then print them out. Then, they can keep their entries in a special section of their three-ring notebooks. When you collect journal assignments throughout the semester, students can remove the newest entries, staple them together, and turn in merely a few pages. This will save you the hassle and strain of having to collect and carry stacks and stacks of spiral notebooks.

Journals can be read in different ways. You might want to use a highlighter to mark passages that you particularly like or use a bright-colored pen to make brief comments. By writing comments, you let your students know that you are reading every word, and they become more serious about the assignment. When you assign a grade, do so only on promptness and completeness, not on grammar, spelling, punctuation, sentence structure, or paragraph organization. Journals are a form of freewriting, and students should be assured that the assignment is an exercise in putting words on paper, not editing and creating polished prose.

If you collect journals at intervals throughout the semester (perhaps three times), the reading is not quite as laborious. Besides, you will discover a wealth of information about your students that will help you understand their frustrations, their motivations, and their other responsibilities. If you are afraid of burning out on journal reading, you can ask students to turn down the corners of a certain number of entries that they would like for you to read and comment on. You can then skim the remaining entries to note them for credit.

Another alternative is to collect journals only at the end of the semester. Ask students to add page numbers, a title for each entry, a table of contents, and an evaluative conclusion. In this way, students can analyze their work and observe their growth as writers throughout the semester.

You can establish criteria for format and content, but the best journals are those in which the student is given free rein to select the topic. Prepare a handout that explains the journal assignment (several samples are included on pp. 99–102) and offer suggestions. Have students read the section on journals in Chapter 5 of *Real Skills*. This section focuses on journals as an idea-generating strategy. Another type of journal is the reading journal, in which students keep a running record of what they are reading and write responses to it. Frank Smith and Mike Rose, among others, point to the value of summarizing, digesting, and recasting something a student has read in his or her own words. When students can process a selection in

this way, they have a certain hold on it—as well as a memory aid for recall and review at exam time. Ideally, students make reading journal entries before, during, and after the actual reading. Before reading, students should write predictions based either on the title and a quick skim or on the first paragraph. During reading, students should note sentences or thoughts that may lead to more writing or that simply interest them. After finishing the reading, students should somehow process the piece as a whole in a response of their own that takes off where the selection ended. (In this chapter, see the Reading Response Guidelines on p. 103, by Jack O'Keefe at Richard J. Daley College in Chicago.) The apparatus in *Real Skills'* readings section, Readings for Writers, meshes well with this approach. The Guiding Question that appears at the beginning of every selection can be used to make a prediction about the work. Questions in the margins of readings encourage further prediction, as well as reflection on the writer's ideas and identification of main points, support, and so on. The follow-up apparatus asks students to summarize and respond to the selection, and includes ideas for paragraph writing.

Journal Writing Tips

A journal is a place to save what you think and feel by recording your reactions, motives, insights, and important ideas. Keeping a journal will not only develop your self-expression but also help you grow as a person. Then, too, it may serve another purpose: It can provide a bank of ideas from which to draw for writing assignments. Professional writers often keep journals for saving details about unusual events they see and interesting conversations they hear. Later they may use the items in articles or books, because they know that true-to-life details give depth and authenticity to writing.

In a journal, you can describe your ideas and emotions without worrying about punctuation, grammar, audience, or evaluation. Your goal is to discover what you really think and feel, to dig down into your mind and let the words flow. Journal writing not only clarifies thinking and fosters creativity but also helps you feel more comfortable in the physical act of writing.

Keep your journal on loose-leaf notebook paper in your three-ring binder, and write in it at least three times a week. You may want to set aside a special place and time, but planning is not necessary. By the end of the semester, your journals will contain at least thirty-six entries. Each should be at least a paragraph in length, clearly numbered and dated. You may either write by hand or use a computer; if you write, please write legibly. Journals will be collected at announced due dates (see class plan), approximately every three to four weeks. Staple your entries together before turning them in.

An additional handout offers some suggestions for journal entries, but I would like for one journal entry a week to be a summary of and reaction to a magazine or newspaper article you have read or a book you have read. You may also react to situations or discussions that have occurred in this class or in any of your other classes.

In order to have the required number of entries, you will need to write in your journal only three times each week.

Suggested Journal Topics

1. React to a movie or TV show that you have seen recently. Give a short summary, then tell what you did or did not enjoy. Evaluate the show or reflect on ideas it made you think about.

2. Name an American city or town that you have visited and tell in detail what it is like. Use as many of the senses (sight, hearing, smell, etc.) as are logical to create an image in the reader's mind.

3. Write a description of your favorite leisure-time activity.

4. Write a narrative paragraph by completing the following statement: *I was never more scared than* . . .

5. Describe what you would like to be doing five years from now.

6. Complete the following statement: *My most unusual teacher was* . . . Explain what made that teacher unusual.

7. What advice would you give a teenage beginning driver?

8. Tell your little sister (brother) how to get out of doing the dishes.

9. Describe a new person you have met. What qualities or characteristics impressed you the most?

10. Write a paragraph that describes your ideal job.

11. How are you different from your family members? In what ways are you like them?

12. Focusing on some current issue, write brief letters to the editor of your campus or local newspaper.

13. Invent a product, and then write four or five complete sentences that highlight its strengths and that convince the readers of a magazine or newspaper to buy the product.

14. Describe your feelings about a class that you dislike. How could it be improved?

15. Describe a class that you like. Why do you like it? How is it different from your other classes?

16. Copy a favorite quotation and explain what it means to you.

17. Record a funny, interesting, or thought-provoking statement. After you record the quote, try to make the idea relate to your own life or thoughts.

18. Write a poem.

19. Complete the following: *I was doing well until* . . . Being specific, describe the situation to your reader.

20. Explain how you would teach this class if you were the professor.

21. Describe your favorite vacation spot.

22. Describe what you like most about yourself.

23. If you could change history, explain what changes you would make.

24. Tell how one person has had an impact on your life.

25. Invent a holiday. Describe when it would appear on the calendar, how it would be celebrated, and why it should be a holiday.

26. Describe a goal you have set for yourself.

27. Recount a dream or daydream.

28. Express any special thoughts or feelings you have had during the day.

Reading Response Guidelines

- Check your prediction after the prereading. Were you on target about what the full reading would say? If not, explain why in a few sentences.

- Summarize the reading in a short paragraph or a longer one if the reading is lengthy.

- What is the author's main point, and how does the author support it?

- Can you relate anything in the reading to your own life or to the lives of those around you? Connecting the reading to your own life may make a good topic.

Sample Reading Journal Entry for Delia Cleveland's "Champagne Taste, Beer Budget"

Prediction: The author will talk about wanting things that are too expensive for you.

Summary: The author tells how she used to be hooked on buying designer clothes. However, she spent so much time and money trying to look good that she started cutting school and got left back in tenth grade. After that reality check, she ended up going to an alternative high school and realized that her focus on material things was preventing her from having real, interesting experiences. Now, she buys reasonably priced clothes and saves her money.

Relate to my life: There is a lot of pressure to buy fancy things to fit in, especially for teenagers. TV shows like *Gossip Girl* make it seem like it's normal to wear designer labels all the time. I know my daughter always wants to run out and spend her paycheck right away. It's hard to get her to understand the value of saving money.

Use the Writing Center

Sometimes, the most useful instructional approach sends students out of the classroom—and to the writing center. Writing centers come in all sizes and philosophies. Some centers fall under the auspices of the English department, a developmental studies area, continuing education, or student services; others are part of a larger learning center or a separate entity. Some centers were established as labs for classes, some serve multiple disciplines, and some are learning centers that offer various review classes in grammar and writing.

Staffing is as varied as support and purpose. Many centers are staffed by a combination of paid and volunteer tutors. Some hire trained professional tutors with at least a bachelor's degree, whereas others rely on faculty who volunteer or who are assigned as part of a teaching or lab load. Many hire peer tutors.

Hours and modes of operation also vary. Some centers operate on a set schedule; their tutors, who are assigned to different areas or teachers, meet regularly with students by appointment. Others, perhaps more commonly, operate on a drop-in basis. Generally, the drop-in arrangement works well because of the unpredictable schedules of students who also work and have family responsibilities. In centers where students can drop in, there is a casual, comfortable atmosphere that can help reduce the tension of a tutoring session. Also, a drop-in arrangement may allow the center to serve more students than other arrangements because students can visit the center on the spur of the moment. However, be aware that limited hours are often a problem—writing centers that are not open at night and on weekends may not fit students' needs.

No matter how they are organized, most writing centers operate under the same general theory: Writing tutors can help students discover their abilities and thus become better writers, not just producers of better writing. For the most part, writing center staff will not give answers; they will only ask questions to help students focus, think, organize, take risks, and demonstrate their critical thinking skills.

If your college has a writing center or tutoring center, make sure your students are aware of it. If possible, take class time to walk your students to the center for a brief orientation. That way, they not only find out where the center is located but also meet the staff. Then they will not feel too uncomfortable when they go for help the first time. Encourage your students to use the support services. Their visits will save you time, and your students also will benefit from hearing directions from another point of view.

Meet with your writing center staff to determine what services are available. Some facilities offer guidance in audience and approach; generally, they will help the student edit, but they will not edit for the student. Some writing centers provide excellent handouts and writing aids that your students can apply to your class and other courses. Other facilities offer tutoring for students who have problems in grammar and writing. Some centers have computers that offer grammar exercises, writing assistance programs, and Internet access.

To ensure a successful experience for your students, you need to work with the staff. Do not send your students to the writing center for help without clear guidance. See if your center has a form that you can send with the student indicating what you want the student to work on. You can also create your own referral form or write specific instructions on the student's paper. Ask if the staff would like you to send copies of your assignments (and samples of completed assignments) so that they know what to expect when your students come in.

Also, be sure the center's staff members know what you expect of them. Do you want the staff to question the student to help him or her find more supporting points? Do you want the staff to merely help with proofreading? Then, follow up on the students you have sent to the center (some centers send monthly reports to faculty regarding which students have visited the center, why, and for how long). By working closely with the staff, you will probably discover that the writing center will welcome you and your students with open arms, and you will all enjoy the relationship.

If your college does not have such a center, you may want to investigate some online writing centers. (See Resources for Developmental Professionals in Chapter 12 of this manual.)

9

Teaching ESL Students and Speakers of Nonstandard English

Revised by James May, Valencia Community College

A Word or Two about Language

Before beginning our discussion of ESL students, it may be a good idea to discuss the general concept of linguistic diversity. As a developmental writing teacher, you are likely to encounter three broad groups in your classes: students who speak standard American English, speakers of English as a second language, and native speakers who speak nonstandard dialects. The majority of this chapter is devoted to the linguistic and cultural needs of your second-language students; however, this beginning section will focus on the needs of students who do not speak standard American English as a native language.

As you read this chapter, you may notice that students who speak nonstandard dialects of English have much in common with second-language learners. Dialects are varieties of language that contrast in pronunciation, grammar, and vocabulary; they are also often associated with geographic areas and social class. Some examples of dialect differences in English include Indian English, Caribbean English, Midwestern English, Bostonian English, Southern English, Appalachian English, and Black English. Some dialect speakers were born in another country and have language influences from that country even though they have lived in the United States for years. These students are sometimes known as "Generation 1.5." Like learning a new language, learning a new dialect is a long, slow process.

Dialects are one of the most interesting features of language, but they are also one of the most controversial, particularly in schools. Speakers of standard English who hear a nonstandard dialect often make erroneous assumptions about the speaker's intelligence and motivation. Teachers of nonstandard-English-speaking students need to recognize that their students' linguistic differences rarely indicate true linguistic incompetence, and that speaking a nonstandard dialect does not impede cognitive development. In fact, years of sociolinguistic research have shown that dialects are not incorrect, but that they are merely different versions of the standard language. Correctness in language is a matter of social acceptability, and claims that some varieties are "proper" and others are "sloppy" reflect biased attitudes rather than true linguistic facts.

Keep in mind that such attitudes can negatively affect your students. Research has shown that a teacher's beliefs about students' abilities can act as a self-fulfulling prophecy. When educators underestimate students' abilities because of the dialect they speak, those students will do less well in school, perhaps as a direct result of the negative expectations. Cultural conflicts can also result from erroneous beliefs about dialect. A teacher who demonstrates a distaste for nonstandard dialects of English runs the risk of alienating students, who may see that teacher as elitist. And if this barrier forms between the teacher and the students, the students may lose interest in conforming to the patterns of standard English and may even become defensive of their dialects. Remember, research has shown that students have turned their backs on schools because what they learn there has conflicted with what they learn from their home cultures.

In addition, the high value that many teachers place on objectivity and explicitness, especially in writing, may conflict directly with the verbal styles of many nonstandard-English-speaking communities.

The following suggestions will help you enhance the learning opportunities for all of your students: standard English speakers, speakers of nonstandard English dialects, and speakers of other languages.

- Model a positive attitude toward all varieties of language and culture. By creating a safe environment that respects all languages and cultures, you will prevent students from feeling a need to defend their linguistic and cultural identities.

- Develop a purpose for learning standard English. Many nonstandard-English-speaking students come from environments where standard English is not used; they may not understand why standard English is important.

- Allow for one-on-one conferences. Students may not know what to do with written feedback. One-on-one conferences allow you to clarify the meaning behind the feedback.

- Provide ample opportunities for students to gain reading experience, which plays an important role in developing writing abilities.

- Provide regular, substantial practice designed to develop meaning and fluency in writing. Good writing takes practice, so spend less time on grammatical form and more time on actual writing. Provide the most feedback about the aspects of students' writing that differ significantly from standard English.

- Make writing assignments realistic. If your students can develop real goals for writing, they may begin to see the benefits. You may also want to provide an opportunity to write for multiple audiences.

- Provide explicit instruction not only of the writing process, but also of learning strategies.

- Use collaborative writing activities that allow students to benefit from seeing other writers at work. Pairing high- and low-level workers can create benefits for both.

- Allow for flexible grading that empowers students to take control of their own fate. Extra-credit assignments that allow students to better their grades through increased effort are effective motivators.

Teaching the ESL Student

ESL students are like native speakers: amazingly diverse. Some are truly interested in learning, and some do not want to put forth any effort. Some will have completed an ESL program, whereas others will have left a program too soon or will have never even been exposed to ESL courses. Even those students who have been exposed to such courses will vary considerably due to differences among ESL programs across the country.

Theories differ on how ESL students should be taught, and a discussion of the various theories of second-language acquisition is beyond the scope of this chapter. However, it may be a good idea to discuss how ESL students should be treated with respect to grading. One theory holds that ESL students working toward a degree in an American college or university should be assessed by the same criteria that apply to native speakers. Proponents of this theory argue that English-speaking students attending a foreign college would not receive special consideration for their lack of language skills and therefore the same should hold true for foreigners studying here. The truth of this contention remains to be seen. Clearly, however, this theory fails to mention the fact that many ESL students in the United States are actually U.S. citizens. Another theory holds that ESL students deserve special treatment and specialized criteria that overlook some of their language problems (idiom, pronoun, and article usage, for example). This approach may sound reasonable, but whether or not it prepares students to function in the real world also remains to be seen.

As a teacher of ESL students, you may want to put yourself in your students' position. What do you believe would be the best approach to learning a new language? What type of instruction would you find most beneficial? How would you like to be graded? Most of us would agree there should be some middle ground. ESL students may require extra help and assistance, but their writing must be acceptable in the real world if they are to succeed in their chosen careers.

Placement and Assessment

Proper placement of students helps both instructors and students, and including an ESL student in a developmental writing class designed for native speakers can create complications for all members of the class. Many of us are not trained to teach ESL students, and many of their writing problems are distinct from those of native speakers. Also, students who are not ready for regular English classes can become discouraged when faced with failure after failure, especially if the class moves too rapidly or does not cover in detail their types of problems. Proper placement is therefore something you will need to consider. If your college has an ESL program, work closely with the director of that program. Find out what ESL classes are available to students, how placement is determined, and how students advance out of ESL courses into mainstream English classes. If policies and processes are not in effect, offer to work with the ESL faculty to establish guidelines. Also, find out if your college will allow you to transfer a student from your developmental writing class into an ESL class within the first week or two of a semester.

Do not, however, attempt to automatically send a student out of your classroom. Determining who should be in an ESL class and who might succeed in a regular English class is not easy, but if you look for certain clues, you can make logical and objective decisions. Ask the student whether he or she has already completed some ESL classes. If so, the student may speak English somewhat fluently. However, be advised that there is a distinct difference between speaking and writing proficiency in English. Like other developmental writing students, ESL students may speak English quite proficiently while lacking literacy skills. The best way to assess your students is to ask for a writing sample and examine it carefully. If the ESL student's writing is filled with organizational errors, grammatical errors, vocabulary problems, and awkward or confusing syntactic structures—that is, if almost every sentence has some type of meaning or syntax problem—then the student probably would benefit from an ESL program instead of developmental writing. The following examples illustrate passages written by students who need to master more skills before they can successfully complete a developmental writing course. All three are filled with errors, and the students' ideas are hard to understand.

No permitted with citizens who living in Texas carry weapon. After all amount accidents, we can realized almost that situation occur are by criminal they usually carrying a weapon with them whenever they go out, an make it happen wherever with anytime they don't scare who they are. The Taxas Police department they really having that problem but they haven't been found the best way to solution yet, after each ocurred to make person who is a victim of the guns. For instant, if the legal of the Taxas absolutely unallowable to selling guns also somehow they get all guns form any stores and controll on they hand. That would help people more safty.

In the United States people legally carry weapon so you can safe by yourself but behind this reason, it makes you feel worry and also have more accident shoot each other. For example, last six months ago in the Plaza area on the Haltom road Da Lat was a place had happened an accident shooting a girl about 17 years old because this girl went with her new boyfriend and she did not break up her old boyfriend yet at that time, two these guys meet each other at that place driving an accident has happened the old her boyfriend had to shooted an minor person.

The social will become unsafely if everybody can legally carry a weapon. It is easy to see on this point. Teenagers can also legally carry a guns, and they can active in anytime on their ages. The ages that make them feeling victory and ready to fighting with everybody; the ages that make them can not control by themselves. Among of them, we have not listed the groups of gangster that is one of the social's worry, and the police on the street.

One of the most obvious problems exhibited by these three samples is a complete lack of organization. Good paragraph construction in English typically follows a specific pattern of organization. As you know, paragraphs typically begin with a topic sentence, which in some way previews a pattern of support. The support points then follow this previewed pattern and relate back to the topic sentence. In the examples above, you may have had a difficult time identifying the topic sentences. Therefore, you had no way of guessing the possible pattern of organization and may simply have moved from word to word, attempting to make meaning out of the whole thing. It is more likely, however, that you got frustrated and stopped reading each paragraph after the first few sentences.

The point here is that these students not only have grammar, vocabulary, and syntax problems but also fail to recognize the organizational pattern of paragraphs in English. When assessing ESL students, keep in mind that different cultures often prefer different organizational patterns. Some cultures allow for more digression in their writing. Others allow for parallel structures—what we would consider redundancies. Still others follow circular patterns that may never mention the topic explicitly.

Not all ESL students write like those who produced the previous three samples. Other nonnative speakers have been in the United States longer, have studied English in their countries, or have immersed themselves in learning English. Their writing will be clearer and will have fewer errors. In fact, you may discover that most of the errors are merely a result of poor proofreading skills. The following examples illustrate passages written by two students who probably can succeed in a regular class. Both examples have errors, but their main ideas are readily understandable. Notice that the topic sentences in these passages are clearer, allowing readers to follow the writer's pattern of logic more easily.

> American citizens should have a right to carry concealed weapons. You never know whats going to happen, when you walk out of your house. The legislature of Texas made a great dession about this National Rifle Association. For an example when you walk out of your house front door, when someone try to mug you would you rather have a concealed weapon to protect yourself or not I would rather to have one and protect myself.

> Many people considered weapon carrying is a good way to protect themselves in any situation. But I oppose that view. I think that people should not legally carry a weapon because it is cause many accidental shootings. First of all, people's lives was threaten by legally carry a weapon. As we know that in society, such as in school, work place, hospital, we always have disagreement while we are argueing. Shooting is a good method to solve this problem. Perhaps, many people who misused gun will take this advantage to show of their power over the crowd that caused killed innocent citizen.

Obviously, the first paragraph is more polished than the second, but both of these students fall within the realm of acceptable writing for a nonnative speaker in a class of native speakers.

Instructional Strategies

Once you have determined which students belong in your class, what do you do with them? Whether you are working with a standard American English speaker, a speaker of a nonstandard English dialect, or an ESL student, your task as a teacher is to help all of your students arrive at the same point: the acquisition of standard American English. A mixture of cultures can be a rewarding experience for you and for your entire class. However, you should not automatically assume that an ESL student knows what you expect of college students in the United States. (Nor should you assume that ESL students know everything about their own culture, since many are American citizens.) Therefore, after you express your expectations orally, you need to provide a written explanation for future reference. This is a safe practice that can be employed with all of your students.

Another way to help ESL students understand American academic culture is to have a class discussion in which students describe their conceptions of the academic expectations of college students. If students have experience studying in colleges abroad, you may want to ask about their academic experiences in those countries. Consider listing the findings on the board and then using that list to compile a written set of expectations for students in your class. This may help you understand your students' mind-sets and determine what assistance you may need to provide to make the transition into your class an easy one. Whether you have an entire ESL class or only one or two ESL students in your class, most students seem to enjoy learning about educational programs in other countries. This discussion also helps the students build a sense of community. By allowing all students to share aspects of their home culture, you can create a culturally inclusive environment in which your ESL students will feel safe to stray from their dependency on their native language.

Encourage students to write about their own experiences and to share their writing with their classmates. However, for students to feel comfortable enough to do so, you will need to model respect toward linguistic differences. Without considering them wrong or deficient, discuss how your ESL students are different so that they can scaffold their learning around those differences. Be careful not to overcorrect your nonnative speakers. Excessive overt correction may lead to a decrease in motivation and a lack of willingness to participate.

Once your ESL students have begun to share their work, watch whom they share with. Often, native speakers will pair off with other native speakers and nonnative speakers will pair off with other nonnative speakers. Assigning an ESL student a native-speaking partner can help both students learn and grow. Recall from Chapter 8 of this manual that active learning is the best form of learning. For a native speaker, teaching a nonnative-speaking partner represents a prime opportunity for active learning. And in some situations, you may find that an ESL student has more background knowledge than the native speaker. For example, if you teach in a computer classroom or lab, you may discover that the nonnative speakers take to the computers beautifully, whereas some of your older native speakers approach the computer with much trepidation. Therefore, although the native speaker may be in a better position to offer guidance on language problems, the nonnative speaker may be in a better position to offer guidance on computer problems.

One area you may choose to be strict about is spoken language. Encourage all your students to speak in standard English while in the classroom. Remind your students that, although you respect their dialect or native language, they must practice standard English in order to learn the language. However, be careful about completely banning their native language from the classroom. If you hear two students conversing in their own language during work time, ask if they are having a problem with the assignment. If they are, then your question gives them the opportunity to ask you in English. If you are trying to explain something to a student and the student does not seem to understand, feel free to ask another student to help you out. Even native speakers will not always understand what you mean, and we sometimes have to ask someone else for another way of explaining the idea. Be prepared to employ multiple approaches for teaching the same concept. If you are not prepared to explain things in more than one way, tell students that you will get back to them when you come up with a more effective way of teaching it.

The classroom should be psychologically comfortable for all students to learn optimally; this is especially true for second-language learners. Many ESL students will feel uncomfortable producing in English unless they feel it is safe for them to do so. One theory even suggests that there is an affective filter that can block language learning unless students are made to feel comfortable and safe. To create a positive learning atmosphere for your ESL students (as well as for your other students), begin by modeling respect of language and culture. Allow students to see that you value their opinions and explanations, especially those that link learning to their own languages and experiences. For more specific suggestions on making your classroom comfortable for all students, see Chapter 3 of this manual.

Remember that in some cultures students must pass only a proficiency test to pass the class. Your students may not be accustomed to daily assignments and homework. Often a short study-skills lecture on the need for continuous repetition and reinforcement can help nonnative speakers understand the value of and the demand for this type of work. ESL students may benefit from explicit instruction of the cultural expectations of American schools. If you present this information at the beginning of the course, most students start out on the right foot. Unfortunately, you still may have a few bright students who resist the idea. However, if you sit down with them and explain that they can complete the course successfully only by following the requirements, most will settle down into the routine. Setting this priority early helps them not only in your class but in other classes as well.

To help ESL students with their writing, emphasize organization and encourage student–teacher conferences. Have students begin any writing assignment with some form of prewriting (freewriting, clustering, brainstorming); then show them how to turn the resulting information into an informal outline. Stress that the outline will help them stay focused on their topic and will relieve some of the pressure of deciding what to say as they are drafting. Provide samples from former students, newspapers, or the text for your students to examine and then follow. When students are ready to move from the drafting to revising, help them check the order of their ideas and use transitions. (See Chapters 7 and 8 of *Real Skills*.)

If your school requires students to perform timed writings, you may want to discuss how the timed writing process differs from the standard writing process. Your ESL students may show a lack of editing skills on timed tests. Remember these students are not writing in their native language and therefore require more time than native speakers do to monitor their output. In addition, your students may benefit from explicit instruction on how to turn prompts into thesis statements.

Many ESL students are extremely bright and know the grammar rules; often, the errors they make are a result of rushing their writing and not taking the time to edit carefully. When you have ESL students who consistently make the same type of error, sit down with them individually and ask them to explain the rule to you. Or have the students read their papers aloud. If they can correct the errors orally, then they understand the rule. In either case, you will know if the problem is due to lack of knowledge about editing or a lack of time. If the problem is due to lack of editing skills, stress the importance of this stage of the writing process.

You may also want to encourage your students to take advantage of the writing centers and tutoring centers on campus. Tutors can give students interactive explanations of their errors, something you may not have the time to provide. However, you may need to explain what kind of help is acceptable and what kind becomes plagiarism. Plagiarism is not an internationally accepted concept. Some cultures even believe that copying someone else's work is a form of respect or flattery.

If you discover that your students do not know the grammar rules, explain the rules in a variety of ways and have students develop several original sentences applying them. Modeling is an excellent way to teach rules to both native and nonnative speakers. For instance, you can give students sample sentences and ask them to follow the same form to write their own sentences. You can go over the sentences with the students to determine if they now understand and can apply the rules to their own paragraphs and essays.

Instead of focusing on everything ESL students are doing wrong, look for aspects of language (plurals, gerund use, etc.) that they are sometimes using correctly. Have them focus on why they have used something correctly under one circumstance and incorrectly under another. Consider marking only one kind of problem in one of their drafts (verb problems, for example). The benefits of this approach are threefold. First, there will be less negative, and potentially discouraging, feedback on students' papers. Second, it will relieve the burden of your having to correct everything, which can be a daunting task. Third, if your ESL students are sometimes applying specific rules correctly and sometimes not, they may be stuck in one stage of development. Therefore, focusing on that stage of development may help them transition through it with greater ease.

How should you help ESL students overcome grammar problems while maintaining the focus of the course? Some ESL errors are common to both native and nonnative speakers and can easily be worked on in class: pronoun reference, subject-verb agreement, and s endings on verbs, for example. Another major problem that both ESL and many native-speaking students face is spelling. If you assign weekly (or daily) spelling words from the list of 100 commonly misspelled words on page 454 of *Real Skills*, you can incorporate both spelling and vocabulary into your students' weekly or daily routine. If you use computers, introduce ESL students to the spell checker. However, warn them about overuse of the thesaurus option. ESL students often fail to recognize the different connotations of English words.

Other problems are more specific to ESL students and require a variety of approaches. Incorrect usage of idioms should be dealt with as the situations arise, by pointing out the problem and explaining the proper use to the student. Some errors may be too complex and time-consuming to tackle in a developmental writing class: verb tenses, definite articles, and prepositions, for example. You should identify the problems and then offer outside assistance, send the student to the tutoring center, or assign individual work outside of class. Some of these typical ESL problems are addressed in Chapter 21 of *Real Skills* and in "language notes" that appear throughout the grammar chapters.

Most developmental students are nonreaders, and many ESL students are likely to fit into that category as well. Make up a list of books or bring old magazines from home. Encourage your ESL students to read the books or magazines and to write in their journals about what they have read. Explain that by reading in English they will learn vocabulary, sentence structure, and idioms. Also, it is important for students to hear standard English. Recommend that they listen to TV and radio news or to audio lessons in a language lab.

Another problem that many nonnative speakers face is a lack of cultural background knowledge. Therefore, you may want to send ESL students to museums, parks, zoos, plays, community centers, hospitals, and the like to complete specific assignments and to report back to the class. In other words, they need 200 percent more exposure to the language and culture than other developmental students do. This is something that native speakers already have, and we as teachers often take for granted.

As you work with your ESL students, remember that just like all the special needs students in your class, they require a multisensory approach to learning. They also need an abundance of modeling to help them understand your expectations and to build their confidence and skills. You must be patient yet demanding, and you must be available to offer individual help if necessary. Although it may sometimes take many attempts before an ESL student understands a concept, if you are nurturing, your students will be motivated. As one instructor pointed out, this may be your student's first class, and his or her experience in the classroom with you and the other class members may determine whether this is his or her last class. Although working with ESL students (or any developmental students) can be trying at times, the rewards are limitless.

10

Assessing Student Writing and Progress

Revised by Karen Eisenhauer, Brevard Community College

Thoughtful evaluation is one of the most important services you offer as a teacher. Your evaluation begins the process of guiding your students, individually, to becoming better thinkers, more discerning judges, and better writers. This is where, as the saying goes, the rubber meets the road. But the task does not have to be painful for you or your students.

When we assess our students' writing, we meet them as individuals. Their writing difficulties may be commonplace or peculiar, but remedying those problems will usually require that we communicate to them as the unique individuals they are. We can recognize and comment on their particular strengths, and we can direct them to the most productive and important areas for improvement. This opportunity to have an individualized impact on each student in the class is an opportunity not offered in many other courses.

However, this "opportunity" can be a great deal of work. For your students, it is a risky undertaking, full of confidence-crushing danger. Fortunately, with some careful consideration of your objectives and thoughtful planning, you can avoid the pitfalls and make your course something that both you and your students look forward to.

Purpose and Philosophy of Assessment

There are two quick stories I would like to relate to you as we begin, incidents that helped me form my basic philosophy regarding the purpose and goal of assessing *any* work done by students. Both incidents occurred when I was a student teacher working with Mrs. Dewey, a woman for whom I

have vast respect: She is the teacher we all aspire to be.

Scene one: A student has not finished her exam during the allotted class period. She is concerned about not having finished and speaks to Mrs. Dewey as she is leaving class. Mrs. Dewey asks the student if she would like to come back during her lunch break to finish the exam. With profound gratitude, the student says that she will return. As she leaves the classroom, the rather naive intern (me) asks Mrs. Dewey if she is not concerned that the student will look up some of the answers to questions between now and lunchtime. Looking down her nose through her bifocals at the intern, Mrs. Dewey replies pithily, "Well, I should hope she would." Silence and chagrin are the response of the intern who suddenly realizes that learning, by whatever method, is the highest priority in this classroom.

Scene two: The intern is sitting in the large, open teachers' workroom when another English teacher comes in carrying an armload of cardboard posters, and plops them on her desk, complaining loudly, "Just look at these. I told the students to make a poster for their book report, and this is what I got." She holds up a plain white poster with three stick figures drawn on it in pencil, an effort that looks as if it were completed on the school bus this very morning. She demands to know, "How am I supposed to grade something like this?" The intern is again silent. She is embarrassed for the teacher standing in front of such disrespectful work. When the intern mentions the incident to Mrs. Dewey, she receives an acerbic response: "You get what you ask for. If you don't ask for much, you won't get much."

These incidents have become vital lessons for me:

- **THE BEST ASSESSMENTS EVALUATE *AND* TEACH.** Assessment, including exams, should not be only for the purpose of awarding grades. Evaluating student progress is useful, but the best assessments should be, primarily, another teaching tool, focusing on learning and improving. Students who care enough to ask for additional time to complete an exam, even though they may look up answers, can usually have a little extra time in my class. They learn more this way.

- **FOR QUALITY RESULTS, MAKE QUALITY ASSIGNMENTS.** Quality assignments are usually not made spontaneously. When students receive an assignment, they need to know what constitutes success. Therefore, you as the instructor must have defined beforehand, in concrete terms, the components of success. And you must share this information with your students.

Making the Assignment

If students are to be successful, they will need a road map, provided by you, on which the destination is clearly marked. This means that you must have a destination chosen ahead of time and be prepared to point out at least one potential route for reaching it. In practical terms, this means that you should plan your assessment strategy as you plan the assignment. And, when you give the assignment to your students, give them the basics of the assessment strategy at the same time.

Providing a road map for assignments does not mean you have to stifle creativity. There are usually many different routes to a single destination, and people will have different preferences for their journey. But regardless of the route, it is critical that everyone understand the destination.

Building assignments and assessments simultaneously requires that you determine which assessment method will work best with the assignment you have in mind. Some of the following considerations should help with these decisions:

- **KNOW WHAT YOU WILL BE LOOKING FOR AS YOU EVALUATE.** Establish the criteria for success and have these clear in your own mind as you build an assignment. It is also useful to have an idea of the relative importance of each criterion. Determine the basic components of a successful essay and make a list, ranking the list in order of importance.

- **ENSURE THAT STUDENTS CLEARLY UNDERSTAND YOUR RESPONSE TO THEIR WRITING.** If they do not understand, they will not be able to learn or improve and your efforts will be wasted. (Some strategies to help in this area are described later in this chapter.)

- **AVOID EXCESSIVE EVALUATION.** Providing too much feedback at once may cause students to become confused or to lose hope. Focus on the most important items first. If a paragraph contains a weak or inadequate topic sentence, what is the use of marking spelling errors?

- **STRESS THAT REVISION IS CRUCIAL TO IMPROVEMENT.** Make revision a normal and expected part of the routine. This will free you from having to mark everything on your first evaluation. For their first few assignments, I tell students that all papers will be revised until they are worthy of an A. (Portfolios are another strategy for dealing with the problems of too much evaluation and revision. Portfolio grading is discussed on p. 129.)

- **REMEMBER TO COMPLIMENT.** Students will work for compliments, and they will remember them longer than criticisms. They are likely to repeat behavior you praise, so make it a point to include a compliment or two.

- **MANAGE YOUR TIME.** Time management is crucial to *your* sanity. Determine what you will grade intensively, what you will check for completion, and what you will let students evaluate in class or on their own. It is not necessary that every piece of work receive a score. Too many grades can also become overwhelming for students as well as for you.

- **PUT SUCCESS WITHIN STUDENTS' REACH.** If papers will be revised until they are worthy of an A, students will feel that success is possible and will have less incentive to cheat.

Communication Strategies

Helping Students Understand Your Evaluation

Have you ever watched a group of students, regardless of the course, as they receive newly graded papers? Even if the grade is on the front, they will immediately scan the rest of the paper for any written comments. Until they have read all comments, it is useless to try to get their attention. Comments are what students truly value in evaluation. Comments, both positive and negative, are what they will remember, and comments are your most powerful tool for guiding improvements. The following strategies may help:

- **BE CONSISTENT IN YOUR USE OF TERMS.** Will you be looking for a main point or a topic sentence? Do you talk about "run-ons" or "fused sentences"? It is usually best to use the same terminology as the text. If you vary from the text, provide students with a means to compare your terminology to that in their books.

- **DISTRIBUTE A CHART OF CORRECTION SYMBOLS.** Students need to know what the editor's marks on their papers mean. Include a sample of your handwriting on the chart so that they can see what your particular marks look like. *Real Skills* includes a chart of correction symbols in its back pages; you can photocopy it with your handwritten marks in the column titled "Your Instructor's Symbol."

- **READ A PAPER THROUGH BRIEFLY BEFORE MARKING IT.** This allows you to determine where you will focus your effort. You should not spend more time evaluating a paper than the student spent in writing it. If the paper lacks unity and coherence or has no main point, note these deficiencies and ignore the other problems until the next revision.

- **USE COLOR TO COMMUNICATE.** I use purple ink for content comments, green ink for grammar errors, red ink for grammar errors they really ought not to be making at this point, and a variety of highlighters for other necessary notes. Disorganized papers, for instance, may end up looking like a rainbow as I highlight each different idea and its companion sentences in different colors. Students soon get the idea that all the orange sentences should be grouped and not sprinkled throughout the paper. A colleague uses pink highlighter for "perfect"—a quick way to provide a compliment. While this may seem time consuming, if you can communicate effectively the first time, you will not have to repeat yourself on every subsequent paper.

- **CONFERENCE WITH STUDENTS BRIEFLY WHEN YOU HAND BACK THEIR PAPERS.** They will not understand everything you have marked, and will probably not ask what you mean, but if they have some individual time with you, they will ask questions. Organize classroom activity to allow for these mini-conferences.

- **CONSIDER MAKING YOUR OWN RUBRIC FOR MARKING PAPERS.** Steps for building rubrics are discussed in detail later in this chapter.

- **PROVIDE PLANNING SHEETS TO BE FILLED IN AS A PREWRITING STRATEGY.** Collect these and look them over. These are frequently helpful in spotting where a student is misunderstanding the writing process. You may also want your students to submit all stages of their writing: brainstorming, freewriting, initial drafts, peer-editing responses, and any additional drafts. This way, you can see where the student began and what thought processes he or she followed. In addition, when you are looking for positive comments, you can refer to the amount of work, the quality of revisions, or the evidence of development. (Note that forms for planning paragraphs are included in *Additional Resources to Accompany Real Skills*.)

- **DO NOT GRADE EVERYTHING.** You can require multiple drafts and grade only the final product. Initial drafts can be read for content only. Secondary drafts can be skimmed for content and organization. Mark grammatical, punctuation, and spelling errors in later drafts. This approach will emphasize writing as a process and will also avoid giving students too much to consider at once. The sidebar on pages 115–116 shows how different versions of a single paper were marked, with comments on grammar and spelling reserved for the last version.

- **CONSIDER USING A COMPUTER.** For example, Microsoft Word has a comment feature, and *Comment,* a Web-based tool available with this book, makes commenting on papers quick and easy.

- **AND REMEMBER THAT SOME ASSIGNMENTS DO NOT REQUIRE GRADES.** Journals, drafts, and workshop materials may simply be checked.

Encouraging Revision

Because learning to write means learning to revise, consider allowing students who score below 70 to revise their assignments. It is also a good idea to put "Rewrite" or "Revise" on the paper rather than a grade. Some teachers promise students that they will grade only from the top, meaning they will score only the final version. A student who takes the time to revise an assignment using the instructor's comments will learn and improve his or her grade.

Staged Marking of Student Papers

This sidebar shows how an instructor commented on three progressively more polished versions of a student paper. The instructor's comments are in bold within the drafts. Notice how the instructor focused first on major content and organizational issues, reserving comments on grammar and spelling for the last draft. This approach can be especially effective for papers that are seriously underdeveloped or error-laden; it keeps the instructor—and the student—from becoming overwhelmed. We begin by presenting the original assignment.

THE ASSIGNMENT: Write a one- to two-page narration essay on an event in your life that taught you a valuable lesson or that changed you somehow, for better or worse. Make sure to use vivid details to bring the event to life for your readers and to show how it affected you. You should check your grammar and spelling before turning in the paper.

DRAFT 1

You might call me "whack," that's fine but its just how I feel. Like one time they were really going at it, me and my sister staid out side because we know what good for us. It was 12:00 at night and dishs braking. **Good! Can you give us more information about this scene? Other sounds, smells, sights?** She said Im not going in there and I said me neither, so we didnt. Fall asleep on the ground but its better then inside. **Why does this particular memory stand out for you? What lesson did you learn from this event?**

So thats why I glad. Like yesterday I feel so happy. My sister saw too. you look so happy she said. Mama scraed it gonna mess wit us but I told her mama do'nt worry it better this way. **Why is the situation better now? Is your home more peaceful without all the fighting?** We hate him do'nt we. My sister shake her head at me, my mama say do'nt say that its not right, he your daddy. I say I do'nt care. She didnt say any thing after that.

I feel happy. Yes.

I asked you to write about an event that changed you. What event are you describing here? Is it the break up of your mother and father's marriage? How might you best introduce this event to your readers? What exactly are you trying to say about it?

DRAFT 2

Can you imagine living in a house where people fighting day and night. **Good hook! But watch your punctuation!** Like one time they were really going at it, I mean my mama and daddy, me and my sister staid out side because we know what good for us. It was 12:00 at night and dishs braking. The bright light coming out our house was red. Mad just like them. No other houses on our street had there lights on. **Thank you for giving me more details. You've painted an excellent picture here. (You can delete the next sentence, which begins with "Ours," because it says the same thing as the sentence before it.)** Our's was the only one. She said Im not going in there and I said me neither, so we didnt. **Who is "she"? Your sister?** Fall asleep on the ground but its better then inside. Its hard to imagine but this happen all the time. Can you blame me for being glad? **Instead of asking a question here, you should make a statement that explains why you are glad your parents' marriage ended.**

Explain in detail two or three things your parents fought about. Also, think of other reasons why you're glad your parents' marriage ended. Write about them in detail.

One day it stoped. I dont know why, it just did. Every think was quiet and peaceful. A bird singing in a tree. I listened to it for a long time. **Great details! Where were you? In the backyard? On the porch? Were you sitting, standing? Also, you should use your dialogue below to write your mother and sister into the moment.** [So thats why I glad. Like yesterday I feel so happy. My sister saw too. You look so happy she said.] **Move this part to your conclusion, since you're reflecting on how you feel after the marriage ended.** Mama scraed it gonna mess wit us but I told her mama do'nt worry it better this way. My daddy was mean and thats all they is to it. Maybe he be buy hisself for a while and he learn something like I did. We hate him do'nt we. My sister shake her head at me, my mama say do'nt say that its not right, he your daddy. I say I do'nt care. She didnt say any thing after that.

I feel happy. Yes.

For the conclusion, tell us exactly how things are better now. Restate what lesson you learned. What lesson do you think your father could learn? What about your mother and sister? Has this experience changed them? How? Will you use the lesson you learned for the rest of your life? How?

DRAFT 3

Can you imagine living in a house where people fighting **(verb tense)** day and night? Like one time they were really going at it, I mean my mama and daddy, **(comma splice)** me and my sister staid **(spelling)** out side **(spelling)** because we know **(verb tense)** what **(word missing)** good for us. It was 12:00 at night and dishs **(spelling)** braking **(spelling and verb tense)**. The bright light coming out of our house was red. Mad just like them **(fragment)**. No other houses on our street had there **(wrong word)** lights on. My sister said, "Im **(punctuation)** not going in there," and I said, "Me neither," so we didnt **(punctuation)**. Fall (verb tense) asleep on the ground but its **(punctuation)** better then **(wrong word)** inside **(fragment)**. Its **(punctuation)** hard to imagine, but this happen **(verb tense)** all the time. I was glad when my mama and daddy got a divorce. Our lives are better without all the fights and stress.

From here on, I haven't marked all the grammar and spelling errors, but there are several of them for you to fix.

The main reason I happy about the divorce was fighting. Sometimes my sister and me didnt think theyed ever quit. Daddy came home late and they fought. Mama buy something daddy didnt think they need and they fought. Its like they couldnt talk, just fight.

Daddy was mad alot. He hated his job and blamed us. When his belt came off me and my sister ran! And when daddy was mad mama was mad too. You didnt have to do much to get hit in those days.

The last thing is we never had any money. Daddy blamed mama and us, but you know I never had any. I dont know where it went. Its not we lived extravigent **(spelling and part of speech—this is an adverb)**. We ate alot of sandwhiches and rice. I be fine if I never have rice in my life! **Great body paragraphs! Your reasoning is clear.**

One day the fighting stoped. I dont know why, it just did. Every think was quiet and peaceful. A bird singing in a tree. I sat in the backyard and listened to it for a long time. Mama and my sister came outside and asked if I was OK. I said yes. She said she scraed it gonna mess wit us but I told her mama do'nt worry it better this way. My daddy was mean and thats all they is to it. Maybe he be buy himself for a while and he learn something like I did. We hate him do'nt we. My sister shake her head at me, my mama say do'nt say that its not right, he your daddy. I say I do'nt care. She didnt say any thing after that. **This paragraph flows much better now.**

So thats why I glad. Like yesterday I feel so happy. My sister saw too. You look so happy she said. I feel happy. Yes. We fight sometimes but its not like before. Daddy got a new job and say his boss is better. Mama likes her job too and we have money now. No more rice or if we do it has meat and gravy. My sister doing good in school. Everything is OK. If any body ask me dont I feel bad because my parents divorce I say no because sometimes people cant live together and be happy. Its better this way. **Good reflection in your conclusion.**

Dear Letitia,

This essay has come a long way. The content and organization are now much better. Thank you for your efforts.
To revise further, you should focus on your grammar and spelling. As I noted, there are several errors after those I marked in the first paragraph. Using *Real Writing* or your handbook, try to correct the remaining errors. Don't hesitate to let me know if you have any questions.

Best,
Professor Reyes

Other teachers believe that once they have read and marked an assignment, they have contributed too much to the assignment for the student to receive full credit. If you want to encourage students to revise on their own, without excessive editorial assistance from you, you could use a scale such as the one on page 123 to determine grades.

My policy has been to require developmental students to revise their first few papers until those papers are worthy of an A. I want them to know just how much work it will take to achieve that goal, and I also want them to know that they are capable of achieving it. With nondevelopmental students, I usually require rewrites for low-scoring papers on the first assignment. In this case, I want students to understand that I am willing and able to help them improve, and to also understand that I do not accept poorly written work.

Criteria for Evaluating Student Writing

As noted previously, you must establish the criteria for success and communicate these to your students. At a minimum, every successful paragraph or essay must have a main-point statement; support for the main point; unity; coherence; and standard forms of spelling, grammar, and punctuation. However, this is not a list students will initially understand. Instead, break this list down into concrete terms you can share with them. *Topic sentence*, for instance, may become *topic and main point about that topic.*

In many states criteria have already been established for you by means of some standardized examination the students will take. If this is the case, obtain a copy of the criteria and base your own criteria on it. Another source to consider for criteria is your text.

Once you have your criteria listed, you will need to decide how you will determine whether the paper meets them. Two common methods of assessment are holistic scoring and analytic grading. In holistic scoring the grader bases the score on his or her impression of the overall quality of the paper. Numerical scores typically range from 1 to 4, or possibly from 1 to 6, but letter grades may also be used. In analytic scoring the grader analyzes and scores the components of the writing. Here the scores can be any sort of point value.

You may use any combination of scoring methods, depending on the assignment you have chosen and your purpose for assessing that assignment. Whichever method you choose, however, remember that it must successfully communicate to students the strengths and weaknesses of each particular work.

Whether you use holistic scoring, analytic scoring, or some other method, a checksheet or rubric of some sort is required in order to maintain consistency and objectivity in the grading process. In each of the sections below, a sample rubric is provided. However, the best rubric for you and your students will be one that you build yourself. Such a rubric will be the one you most thoroughly understand and will therefore use most effectively. It will also be far easier for you to explain the scoring process to your students when you are using your own instrument. The following sections present some common methods of holistic and analytic grading; after these, the chapter gives steps for building your own rubric.

Holistic Scoring

With holistic scoring, the grader reads through the student's work and appraises it as a whole according to a set of general criteria. The criteria address the quality of the essential elements of a paper: topic sentence or thesis, development, organization, logic, mechanics, and usage. A basic method of holistic scoring merely assigns an overall score of 1, 2, 3, or 4 according to the quality of these elements. There is a set of criteria for each possible score, and the grader matches the overall quality of the paper to one set of criteria to determine the score.

While holistic scoring is a tremendous time-saver for the teacher, to students it appears almost completely subjective unless they fully understand the criteria. Even if they do understand, the numerical score alone will not help them improve their writing. A further drawback is that it is difficult for one person to maintain consistency throughout a set of papers.

Holistic scoring is most often used by groups of teachers who get together to grade preliminary or end-of-semester placement paragraphs or essays from a whole set of classes. The teachers begin the scoring session by discussing the criteria and grading a set of control paragraphs or essays that represent the range of point values. The purpose is to have everyone apply the criteria in the same manner. Next, each paper to be scored is read by two graders, who must score them within a point of each other. If a paper receives more than a one-point separation, the paper is read by a third "master" grader. Many colleges report that this method of holistic scoring does provide a clear indication of students' abilities and that, amazingly, the scorers are seldom off by more than a point even when each grader cannot put aside his or her own writing priorities or prejudices.

If your school scores final paragraphs or essays holistically, it will be helpful to your students if you score some of their papers in this manner so that they will develop and understand what constitutes a passing paper. An easy way to manage this effort is to attach a copy of the criteria sheet to the paper and highlight each statement you believe applies to the paper. Some students may have one statement highlighted in each area.

The sample scoring guides on pages 119 and 121 illustrate two approaches to holistic scoring.

A good paragraph or essay has an overall unity: a clear statement of purpose, and a continued focus on that purpose; a clear and semilogical progression of points and/or ideas with clear, semilogical, and specific development; and a sense of closure.

+ means excellent; *3* means adequate; – indicates weakness; *x* means not evident

_____ **Appropriateness:** Does the paragraph or essay adequately address the topic? Are the language and style appropriate to the audience stated in the prompt?

_____ **Unity/Focus:** Is a main idea or statement of purpose clear? Is a focus on that idea maintained throughout the sample?

_____ **Development:** Is the development appropriate to the topic and purpose? Is it adequately applied to a given point or idea? Is there enough of it?

_____ **Organization:** Is organization announced and adhered to, OR is it implied and then logically "unfolded" in some sort of order in the sample?

_____ **Sentence Structure:** *Overall:* Do the sentences effectively communicate an idea, or does grammar hold them back? *Specifically:* Do fragments, comma splices and run-ons, faulty parallelism, subject-verb agreement, pronoun reference (not number agreement), or dangling/misplaced modifiers seriously detract from the paper's quality?

_____ **Usage:** Are there errors in word choice, including homonym transposition (to/too/two, etc.), pronoun number agreement, errors in the use of negatives, ineffective repetition, or tense shifts?

_____ **Mechanical Conventions:** Are there problems with spelling, punctuation, or capitalization?

A graded paragraph or essay receives a score of 1 to 4; paragraphs or essays that score 3 or 4 pass; those that score 1 or 2 do not. Occasionally, a paragraph or essay will receive a 0.

0   The paper is not written in English, does not mention anything remotely close to the topic at least once, or is totally illegible.

1   The paper makes some reference to the topic but is weak in all areas.

2   The paper has weak organization (no logical flow) AND lacks adequate development. Grammar errors occur in almost every sentence, or there are two or more types of major errors that distract the reader.

3   The paper makes sense. It may start off weak but ends on a strong note (or vice versa). There may be some grammatical errors but no distracting ones.

4   The paper is well formed, has a clear focus, and has few errors.

Sample Evaluation Guide—Holistic Scoring (Option 2)

4— Good to Excellent Paragraph or Essay
Organization and Development
- clearly established main idea
- good development with specific examples
- logical organization
- clear understanding of assignment

Sentence Structure
- sentence variety
- few major sentence errors

3— Passing Paragraph or Essay
Organization and Development
- established central point (but weaker than a 4)
- attempt at organization and development
- adequate supporting details
- possible lapses in logic
- clear understanding of assignment

Sentence Structure
- attempts sentence variety
- weaker control over sentences than a 4

2— Needs Remediation
Organization and Development
- unclear or misdirected central point
- some development but some irrelevant points
- few organizational skills
- assignment not fully addressed

Sentence Structure
- little or no sentence variety
- some problems with major sentence errors (fragments, run-ons, comma splices)

1— Needs Remediation (perhaps ESL)
Organization and Development
- no discernible central point
- lack of development
- little if any connection to assignment

Sentence Structure
- seriously flawed
- numerous major sentence errors (fragments, run-ons, comma splices)

Analytic Grading

In analytic scoring, each criterion you have defined—for example, the presence of a topic sentence or thesis statement—is evaluated separately and converted to points. Totaling the points results in a percentage grade. Some instructors find comfort in the precision of numerical grades, while others shy away from such specificity.

When points are used, it is also necessary to determine how many points you wish to award for each item. Will an excellent topic sentence or thesis statement be worth 5 points and a poor one 2 points? Is an excellent topic sentence or thesis worth more points than the effective use of transitions? Taking the time to make these judgments may seem tedious, but it is a valuable exercise that will help you understand what you are actually doing as you evaluate.

Some teachers may be tempted to take off a certain number of points for each fragment or other serious errors, but unless you allow rewrites, you may want to avoid such an approach; think how demoralized a student would feel to receive a –50.

Marking points without explanations is also not an effective means of communicating with students. They will not understand, for instance, why their topic sentence or thesis statement is worth only 2 points while their neighbor's is worth 5. Comments should be included to help students understand the reasons for the score.

The following sections discuss percentage scoring and grid scoring, two common types of analytic grading.

PERCENTAGE SCORING. One popular analytic format is to divide the assignment into five elements and assign a percentage of the total points to each.

- Focus, with a clearly defined topic and relevant details (20%)

- Content that is well developed, with details and original ideas (25%)

- Organization that moves logically and smoothly from beginning to end (25%)

- Style that is appropriate for audience and topic (15%)

- Mechanics demonstrating an understanding of grammar, punctuation, and spelling rules (15%)

A second method looks like holistic grading but uses the criteria set to award percentages rather than whole numbers. The sample percentage scoring guide on page 125 illustrates this method of evaluation.

If you use percentage scoring and allow rewrites, you may wish to adopt a scale such as the following to encourage the best effort right from the start.

Grades on first effort:
90–100 = A
80–89 = B
70–79 = C
0–69 = R
(Rewrite)

Grades on second effort:
85–100 = B
70–84 = C
0–69 = R
(Rewrite)

Grades on third effort:
70–100 = C
0–69 = R
(Rewrite)

Although this scale assumes that students will be allowed to rewrite until they have produced at least a C paper, you may want to give a final grade below 70 if the student's work has not adequately improved by the third effort.

GRID SCORING. Some instructors avoid the problems of assigning grades by using a grid to analyze a piece of writing. Grids are simple checklists that divide the assignment into criteria and distinguish among "Strong," "OK," or "Weak." Grids have the advantage of being quick and nonpunitive. However, if you need to assign grades at the end of the semester rather than give a pass/fail indication, then you can convert the adjective to numbers. Grids may also not work for all assignments. Successful use of grids must also include comments explaining how or why the writing is strong or weak.

Although grids can be redesigned with each assignment, the sample on page 127 is a useful example.

Sample Evaluation Standard—Percentage Scoring

Grades on written work range from A to F and are based on content and form.

90–100   The **A** paper engages the reader's interest and shows strength in all areas of composition: clear, logical ideas; original thought; careful word choice and effective phrasing; no serious errors; and concentration on a main purpose, with strong development and support.

80–89   The **B** paper shows strength in most areas of composition: a clearly stated central purpose; logical and adequate development; and few serious or careless errors. Although showing competence, the B paper lacks the original thought and style that characterizes the A paper.

70–79   The **C** paper is a satisfactory composition with a worthwhile central idea. Although it may be organized clearly and logically, its paragraphs may not be as fully developed as those in the B paper. It avoids serious or careless errors in the use of English and may, in fact, have few correction marks on it, but it lacks the vigor and clarity of thought and expression to be considered above average.

60–69   The **D** paper indicates below-average achievement in expressing ideas correctly, sensibly, and effectively. Most D papers contain serious errors and fail to present a central idea or to develop it adequately. With more careful proofreading as well as fuller and more logical development, many D papers could receive a C.

Below 60   The **F** paper may have one or more of the following problems: serious errors in grammar, spelling, punctuation, and sentence structure; a missing or vague main idea; incomplete development or lack of specific support; failure to follow directions; or plagiarism.

SERIOUS ERRORS:

(1)   Inadequate statement of main idea
(2)   Inadequate or illogical paragraph development
(3)   Awkward sentence structure
(4)   Sentence fragments
(5)   Run-ons or comma splices
(6)   Lack of subject-verb or pronoun agreement
(7)   Problems with verb form or verb tense
(8)   Severe punctuation problems

Errors in any one of these categories can drop your paper one letter grade.
Errors in any two of these categories can drop your paper two letter grades.
Errors in any three of these categories can drop your paper three letter grades.

Sample Evaluation Standards—Grid Scoring

	Strong	OK	Weak
Content, insights, thinking	_____	_____	_____
Genuine revision: substantive changes—not just editing	_____	_____	_____
Organization, structure, guiding the reader	_____	_____	_____
Language: sentences, wording, voice	_____	_____	_____
Mechanics: spelling, grammar, punctuation; proofreading	_____	_____	_____
Overall impression	_____	_____	_____

Portfolios

A portfolio is a selective collection of a writer's work that is assembled for the purpose of assessment. One big advantage of using portfolios, according to Jack O'Keefe of Richard J. Daley College in Chicago, is that instructors can defer grading. Rather than grade each new paper with a number or letter grade, teachers can make comments on the papers and ask for revisions; students do not have to be afraid of a bad grade and negative input. Deferring grades may well encourage students to take more chances with their writing. Developmental writers are often afraid to write, afraid to make mistakes. If writing errors are not judged in a punitive way but are seen as a necessary part of becoming more fluent, students may improve their attitude toward writing and learn that communicating meaning, not avoiding error, is the goal of writing.

At some point in the semester, such as at midterm, the teacher can confer with each student and assign a grade to the portfolio for all papers written to that point. Include in the portfolio the prewriting and earlier drafts, all showing evidence of the student's hard work and reminding him or her that writing is a process, not a one-time event.

If you plan to incorporate portfolios into your curriculum, you should evaluate carefully the different forms this approach can take. Consider the following, keeping in mind the experiences of colleagues in your department who have used portfolios before and any requirements your department may have.

CONTENT. Identify the purpose of the portfolio. Do you want it to foster development, to demonstrate achievement, to show various ways of thinking/knowing/learning (quantitative or qualitative), or to encourage students to make connections among disciplines? Content varies, depending on the purpose of the portfolio. Often, it includes examples of various strategies and can include writings based on personal experiences, social issues, or readings. Students need to be aware of the content requirements from the beginning of the semester. Also, decide how much to include. For instance, you may not want to include any drafts, or you may ask for one assignment with all drafts, with complete annotations.

SELECTION. Decide who will determine the portfolio's contents: student, instructor, college. Will the selection be based on personal likes and dislikes, on established criteria, or on representative samples for certain categories?

REFLECTION. Reflection, a self-analysis of what the student has accomplished, can take various forms: a table of contents, a letter of introduction, a reflective paragraph or essay on the entire semester, an annotation for each item, or a reflection on a single piece of work. Research shows that weak writers do better with a structured experience.

COMMUNICATION. Identify the criteria for success. Are you seeking evidence of connections made among disciplines, of the student's becoming more responsible for his or her own learning, or of the student's readiness for the next course? Clearly communicate the criteria to your students.

EVALUATION. Identify the means of assessment (letter of response, scoring guide, or dichotomous scale) as well as the approach (holistic or analytic). Although many colleges/instructors champion holistic grading, Peter Elbow recognizes a built-in problem with the approach. Because each student's portfolio is unique, comparing all writers and their diverse selections on a single quantitative scale may not work well. For instance, how does one compare a strong narrative and a weak illustration paragraph with a strong illustration paragraph and a weak narrative? Granted, if all selections are strong or all are weak, graders can easily agree on "Excellent" or "Poor/Unsatisfactory" ratings, but the middle-range portfolios with the inconsistent paragraphs or essays prove the most challenging. However, if your only purpose is to determine which students can progress to the next level, which need to remain in remediation or enter remediation, or which will receive scholarships or awards, then holistic grading is efficient and fast.

For more information on teaching with portfolios, see Chapter 11 of this manual.

Self-Assessment

Find ways for students to participate in their own assessment. Not only does this foster active learning and a sense of responsibility, but it allows you to negotiate criteria for assessment that seem fair and relevant to everyone. Midway through the semester, and then again at the end, you may want to have students write a paragraph about what they have gained from the course so far and what they still want to master.

Consider letting students help establish the criteria by which they will be evaluated. At some point in the first week, have students form small groups and ask each group to brainstorm a list of course requirements, letting them know that whatever criteria the class as a whole comes up with will be used to evaluate them at the end of the semester. You may need to provide a few examples of what you mean (e.g., arrive on time, help others in the class, be creative), but let the lists be their own. Combine the lists and distribute the combined list to the entire class at the next class meeting, encouraging discussion of any criteria that seem unclear. Remind students that this list will be part of their final evaluation and that they will have to give themselves a grade. Throughout the semester, check in with individuals and the class to see how aware they are of the list and to ask whether anything should be changed. At the end of the semester, have students assign themselves a grade or a score based on how well they did; they can also write a one-paragraph description of how well they fulfilled the requirements.

You can also have students write self-evaluation paragraphs or essays at the end of the semester; this assignment often works well in combination with portfolios. Students should review any goals they set for themselves at the beginning of the course and look over their work for the entire semester. They can then comment on their worst piece of writing (why they think it is the worst, what about the process or the assignment made it turn out so poorly), their best piece of writing, their strengths and weaknesses as a writer, and what areas of their writing they intend to improve.

Building Your Own Rubric

A rubric that you design yourself can combine features from all the assessment methods listed above and become a valuable, personalized teaching tool. Essentially, it is a checklist for which you have determined which items will be evaluated, and how. A standard rubric allows students to become thoroughly familiar with the qualities you expect to find in their papers, and to chart their progress over time. Students also tend to view this method as more objective than grading done without a rubric.

Building a rubric can be a valuable exercise for you because it forces you to list, in black and white,

the exact criteria for success, and to then adhere to those criteria when grading. Having such a checklist is also helpful for maintaining focus on the selected criteria, thus keeping grading more consistent.

Sample rubrics have been included throughout this chapter, but building your own is a much better idea than copying one. It will be custom-made to suit your teaching style, it will contain your language and your values, and it should therefore be the best means you have for communicating your assessment methods to your students.

To build your own rubric, complete the following steps:

1. **LIST ALL ITEMS YOU WILL LOOK FOR WHEN GRADING.** This list should include all the basic parts or papers, such as a main-point statement, supporting points, development through details, and so on. It may also include other ideas you are emphasizing in class, such as use of transitions.

2. **PLACE CRITERIA IN THEIR ORDER OF IMPORTANCE.** My favorite rubric begins with the items "focused topic" and "main point."

3. **COMPARE YOUR LIST WITH ANY MANDATED RUBRICS.** If your state or school has mandated rubrics, make sure your students will be prepared for any required evaluations at this level.

4. **REVIEW THE SAMPLE RUBRIC IN THIS CHAPTER.** If there are any additional ideas you like in the sample, add them to your rubric.

5. **DETERMINE AN EVALUATION SCALE.** Decide how you will evaluate each item on your list. Is a simple "yes—it is present" or "no—it is not present" sufficient? Or do you want to indicate some sort of quality ranking?

6. **FORMAT YOUR LIST.** Put your criteria in a user-friendly format. Include space for compliments and for specific suggestions for revision.

The sample rubric on page 131 is designed primarily for yes/no evaluation, with space to explain weak areas, if necessary. This rubric assumes that revision will occur several times. Points can be attached to each item, or the comments can stand alone with a grade of R being the grade of record until the paper is satisfactory.

Sample Custom Rubric

Grade for *first writing:* _____

Grade for *first revision:* _____

Grade for *second revision:* _____

Is the topic narrow or focused enough?

Is there a main point that can be *shown, explained,* or *proven*?

Are there supporting statements that *show, explain,* or *prove* the main point?

Are the connections between the supporting statements and the main point clear?

Do the supporting statements have enough details to make them convincing?

Is the information in the paper presented in a logical order?

Are there any detours in the paper?

Are there any sentence fragments?

Are there any run-ons or comma splices?

Are there any spelling errors or other word errors?

Congratulations for:

Suggestions for improving your paper:

Considerations for Statewide Standardized Tests

THEA

If you live in Texas, then you will need to consider the Texas Higher Education Assessment (THEA), formerly the Texas Academic Skills Program (TASP). Students who are not eligible for an exemption or a waiver must take the THEA before enrolling in Texas public colleges and universities. They must pass the THEA in order to receive an associate's degree or certain certificates from a two-year college.

The test has four sections: math objective, reading objective, writing objective, and essay. The objective portion of the writing section measures the student's ability to recognize purpose and audience; unity, focus, and development in writing; effective organization in writing; effective sentences; and edited American English usage. Students are asked to read several short essays and answer forty or so multiple-choice questions about word choice, organization, support, development, grammar, and sentence structure. The essay portion requires students to write an essay of 300 to 600 words on an assigned topic. The essay is graded holistically on its effectiveness in communicating a whole message to a specific audience for a specific purpose.

THEA essays are scored on a scale of 1 to 4 according to the following criteria: appropriateness, unity and focus, development, organization, sentence structure, usage, and mechanical conventions. Essays are scored by two readers who are trained and whose scoring is continually calibrated during the grading sessions. If readers are more than one point apart, then the essay is read a third time and the readers are evaluated to see if one is scoring too high or too low. Scores from both readers are added to give a final score of 2 to 8. If a student scores 4 or lower, the student does not pass the THEA and is required to take developmental courses in order to remain in college. A student who scores 6 or better automatically passes the THEA and continues in regular college courses. If a student scores a 5, the objective test score is considered: Students who score at least 70 percent on the objective test pass the THEA, and those who score lower than 70 percent will need to take developmental courses.

The essays of all students who do not pass the THEA are then analytically scored so that students know what areas they need to improve. By state law, students who do not pass the THEA remain in remediation until they pass that particular section of the test. (However, a recent regulation gives colleges the option of allowing students who pass a school's remedial sequence without passing the THEA to attempt freshman composition. If the student earns at least a B in the composition course, the student is considered THEA-passed.) Additionally, if a student stops attending his or her remedial class, he or she is dropped from all classes. The state administers the THEA several times a year, and a computerized version is also offered. Some schools allow students who pass the THEA during a semester to receive automatic credit for the remedial course in which they are enrolled. Then, the students have the option of continuing to attend class or not returning for the remainder of the semester. A surprising number of students continue with the class to better prepare themselves for their credit courses.

Because the essay generally determines whether the student passes the THEA, your best approach to preparing students for the test is to emphasize the planning and organization of their essays. You might direct students to Chapter 9 of *Real Skills*. Of the seven criteria, four center on the organizational/content areas of the essay. Only three deal with grammar, usage, spelling, and punctuation. Therefore, even if students are weak spellers or do not know a comma from a semicolon, they still have an opportunity to pass the THEA if they can demonstrate an understanding of how to construct a persuasive essay.

To prepare students for the essay portion of the THEA, I would suggest that you begin the course with paragraph writing. A student who does not understand the concepts of topic sentence, specific and relevant support, and summary statement will not be able to write a passing essay. Because the basic structure of an essay is an exploded paragraph, students learn the basics (and teachers evaluate the writing) without the frustrations of hundreds of words and a multitude of sentences that do not blend smoothly. In fact, some instructors spend most of the semester on the paragraph and introduce the essay only during the final three weeks, yet the students have the concepts down so well that essays come more easily. I personally spend half the semester with grammar and paragraphs and do not begin the essay until midterm.

Give students plenty of practice writing THEA-style essays. Here are two sample prompts:

- When patients are in life-or-death situations, should they (or their family members) retain the right to make decisions about whether special measures should be taken to sustain life, or should doctors retain this right? Patients' rights advocates claim that an individual's right to choice does not cease when that person enters a hospital or becomes seriously ill. They believe that doctors and hospitals sometimes want to play God and do not necessarily understand a patient's will to live or wish for no extraordinary treatment measures. Those who believe that doctors should retain the right to decide a patient's treatment say that doctors—with their medical experience and knowledge of a patient's history—are in the best position to make this decision. They say that some families of seriously ill or injured patients give up too soon, while others hold on with false hopes. What is your opinion? Write a letter to the editorial editor of your local newspaper stating and defending your position with logical reasons and evidence.

- You are part of an advisory committee for your state board of education, which has been informed that the state is considering funding fully online schools. In these schools, instruction would take place entirely through the Internet, e-mail, and other online means. Proponents of the schools argue that they would allow better access to education to people living in rural areas, to those with extended or unusual work hours, and to working parents, among others. Opponents say that face-to-face interaction between students and teachers, and among students, is essential to socialization and learning; therefore, online schools would never offer a complete educational experience. In an essay to be read by your fellow committee members, discuss the advantages and/or disadvantages of the proposed online schools. Be sure to provide evidence for your choices.

CLAST

The College Level Academic Skills Test (CLAST) is intended to ensure that students in Florida's public colleges and universities receive uniform, quality education. All college sophomores in Florida must demonstrate competence in writing, language skills, reading, and mathematics before graduating with an associate in arts degree or entering an upper-division program at a state university. The CLAST is one of four ways to demonstrate competence. If all four subtests are taken, the exam lasts four hours, with an additional hour required for check-in, test distribution, and a break. The test is given three times a year at colleges across the state. Students can pick up an exam schedule at their school.

The CLAST includes four subtests: an essay; a multiple-choice test covering word choice, sentence structure, and mechanics (punctuation, spelling, and grammar); a reading test; and a mathematics test. Use the following table in connection with your text to help your students prepare for the essay test and the objective English skills test. The following table lists on the left side the specific skills the CLAST asks students to demonstrate; on the right, you will find the relevant chapters of *Real Skills* that your students can use for review and practice.

Florida College Basic Skills Exit Test

Another state-mandated test in Florida is the Florida College Basic Skills Exit Test, which students in college preparatory classes must pass before enrolling in college-credit courses in English, mathematics, or general education. The test covers reading, writing, and math, and the writing portion has two components: a multiple-choice test and a writing sample, consisting of a paragraph or essay that students must write within fifty minutes.

From Practice to Mastery, a student study guide that can be packaged for free with *Real Skills,* provides pre- and post-tests—and plenty of practice items—to help students prepare for both the reading and writing portions of the test. The list on page 137 shows the writing skills covered on the exit test (and in *From Practice to Mastery*). On the right, you will find the relevant chapters of *Real Skills* that your students can use for review and practice.

CLAST Essay Skills Subtest

SKILL   **Chapter in *Real Skills***

The composition must give evidence that the student

	Skill	Chapter
1.	Determines the purpose and the audience for writing	4
2.	Selects a subject that lends itself to development	5
3.	Limits the subject to a topic that can be developed within the requirements of time, purpose, and audience	5, 9
4.	Formulates a thesis or main idea statement	6, 8, 9
5.	Provides adequate supporting details	6, 8, 9
6.	Arranges the ideas and supporting details in a logical pattern appropriate to the purpose and focus	6, 8, 9
7.	Writes unified prose with relevant supporting material	6, 8, 9
8.	Writes coherent prose with effective transitions between parts	6, 8, 9
9.	Avoids slang, jargon, cliché, and pretentious expressions	25
10.	Uses a variety of sentence patterns	22–23
11.	Avoids overuse of passive construction	15
12.	Maintains consistent point of view	20
13.	Revises, edits, and proofreads for clarity, consistency, and conformity to standard American English	7–9, 10–32

Word Choice Skills

	Skill	Chapter
14.	Uses words that convey the meaning required by context	25
15.	Avoids wordiness	25

Sentence Structure Skills

	Skill	Chapter
16.	Places modifiers correctly	19
17.	Coordinates and subordinates sentence elements	22–23
18.	Uses parallel expressions for parallel ideas	24
19.	Avoids fragments, run-ons, and comma splices	11–12

Grammar, Spelling, Capitalization, and Punctuation Skills

	Skill	Chapter
20.	Uses standard verb forms	14–15
21.	Maintains agreement between subject and verb, pronoun and antecedent	13, 17
22.	Uses proper case forms	17
23.	Uses adjectives and adverbs correctly	18
24.	Avoids inappropriate verb tenses	14–15
25.	Makes logical comparisons	18, 24
26.	Uses standard spelling, punctuation, and capitalization	27, 28–31, 32

Florida Exit Test Writing Skills

SKILL	Chapter in *Real Skills*
1. Identifying topic sentences and thesis statements	6, 8, 9
2. Identifying adequate and relevant support	6, 8, 9
3. Arranging ideas in a logical pattern	6, 8, 9
4. Using effective transitional devices	6, 8, 9
5. Choosing appropriate words or expressions	25
6. Identifying confused or misused words	25–26
7. Using modifiers correctly	18–19
8. Using coordination and subordination correctly	22–23
9. Understanding parallel structure	24
10. Avoiding fragments	11
11. Avoiding run-ons and comma splices	12
12. Using standard verb forms	14–15
13. Avoiding inappropriate shifts in verb tense	20
14. Making subjects and verbs agree	13
15. Making pronouns and antecedents agree	17
16. Avoiding pronoun shifts in person	17
17. Maintaining clear pronoun references	17
18. Using proper case forms of pronouns	17
19. Using adjectives and adverbs correctly	18
20. Using appropriate degree (comparative and superlative) forms for adjectives and adverbs	18
21. Using standard spelling	27
22. Using standard punctuation	28–31
23. Using standard capitalization	32

Conclusion

As the previous sections indicate, multiple-choice writing and grammar questions are a standard feature of many standardized tests. To help students prepare for such tests, consider creating tests and quizzes from *Testing Tool Kit: A Writing and Grammar Test Bank* CD-ROM, available with *Real Skills*. A guide that correlates chapters in *Real Skills* with items in this test bank appears on the inside front cover of this book. Note also that additional tests are available in *Additional Resources*. To prepare students for all types of exams, consider referring them to Appendix A of *Real Skills,* Succeeding on Tests.

When it comes to assessing writing, no method of evaluation is perfect, primarily because no one method communicates to all students. Accept that regardless of the method you choose, personal communication, although time-consuming and labor-intensive, will always be best. Design evaluation to include a manageable mix of personal communication and standardized responses. Try to incorporate time for individual conferences — even two-minute ones — into your class schedule. Plan a group activity and pull students aside one at a time. Invite the writing tutor or perhaps a colleague to come to your class for half an hour to supervise the group work if possible. A calm and relatively stress-free instructor is a better instructor, always.

And regardless of your best-laid plans, inevitably a student, class, or situation will come along that just refuses to mold itself to your design. In that case, be flexible and be creative. One semester, for example, I had a class that would not function cohesively. There were too many distractors and too much bad chemistry. In order to salvage the situation, I put the entire class on individual study for the rest of the semester, providing packets of handouts and assignments to be completed. I did not like it, but it was the best I could manage under the circumstances.

Assessing student writing is challenging. It is part skill, part art, but always a labor of love.

11

Using Writing Portfolios

Craig Kleinman, City College of San Francisco

What Is a Student Portfolio?

Portfolio keeping can greatly enhance learning and teaching as well as program assessment provided it is structured in a way that allows for reflection and communication. This is especially true in a developmental writing course, in which students with little or no experience writing academic essays need to embrace writing as a process and reading as an interactive event, and teachers need to see as much evidence of learning as possible. End-of-course process or learning portfolios enable teachers to help students recognize how much they have learned and grown as writers. Portfolio assessment offers teachers the opportunity to analyze the logic of course sequence and their understanding of students' course entry and exit skills, as well as the efficacy of writing and reading assignments designed for those courses.

But what exactly is a portfolio? A portfolio is a representative collection of a student's writing that "engage[s] students in a process of inquiry into what they have learned" while also "demonstrating the outcomes of learning" (Zubizaretta 28). Portfolios, provided they promote communication, process, and reflection, allow students to transcend the nuts and bolts of specific tasks and mechanical submission. When students develop an awareness and then a critical understanding of why they have been assigned specific tasks and why they are making specific choices during revision, what they learn will likely resonate with long-term meaning, especially when they can clearly convey the significance of what they have done. More and more colleges now use portfolios to determine upper division writing competency instead of an exam, and it is not un-

usual to find portfolios where a master's thesis may have been in the past.

Portfolios are also, of course, very much a part of the world outside the classroom. Photographers, contractors, musicians, dancers, architects, investors, designers, chefs, and a wide range of artists, administrators, and business professionals rely heavily upon portfolios to document and attract work. Teachers, as you may know all too well, are often required to maintain a teaching portfolio as part of tenure review, and many teachers may also create portfolios to (1) store successful or promising assignments, handouts, lesson plans, syllabi, and student work; (2) prepare for future job searches; and (3) share material with colleagues during curriculum development and assessment meetings. You might want to point out the real-world uses of the portfolio when you introduce the idea to your students at the beginning of the course.

Creating a Student Portfolio

Introducing Students to the Portfolio

When introducing the idea of a portfolio, ask if anybody in the class has put one together in the past. Some students will likely raise their hands, mentioning portfolios they have created in high school or other college courses. It is not unusual for students to say that they kept a poetry and prose portfolio or maybe a portfolio of designs or ads created in a graphics class. Ask them why their teachers required them to keep a portfolio. Likely they will say, "To show what we could do." Not a bad answer, but ask them to go further.

- **Ask them how they decided which pieces to add.** Do not be surprised if many of the students say that they made no choices, that they just put everything from that semester or year into a folder. That, arguably, is not a portfolio; it is a sack, maybe even a dumpster. Point out that selection process can make a crucial difference in the quality of the final portfolio.

- **Ask them whether their view of the course, and what they accomplished in it, changed as they reviewed and evaluated their collection of work.** Discuss the benefits of selective revision and metacognition. A college composition course using a text such as *Real Skills* may be the first venue in which a student will be pushed into reflecting critically and examining *why*. Too often students do not have to think critically, and too often this is because they are so disconnected from the academic work required of them. So why not push them to examine the why's of their own rhetorical choices and discursive strategies?

- **Ask them what, in their opinion, are the advantages and disadvantages of a course that requires a portfolio, as opposed to a final exam.** It is likely that few students will actually prefer a final exam. Be sure to stress, however, that creating a portfolio is not less work than a final—it is a different (and for some of us, a more meaningful) way of measuring what was achieved over the course of a semester.

First Steps

REQUIRE STUDENTS FROM THE START OF THE SEMESTER TO MAINTAIN A WORKING FOLDER OF POTENTIAL PIECES FOR INCLUSION. Emphasize the fact that these pieces should show an evolution in the student's use of strategies, approach to a topic, or something similar—they should not simply be a collection of pieces that received the student's highest grades. Ideally, this will motivate students to think more about the revision process and what they should value in teacher feedback.

ESTABLISH A SCHEDULE OF STUDENT–TEACHER CONFERENCES. In working with students to create portfolios, periodic twenty-minute conferences, or perhaps a longer conference with a small group of students, can be more productive than hours of written comments generated in isolation. Conferences can reinforce students' awareness of audience, not to mention showing students that teachers care about their portfolio and are invested in the process.

In their extremely helpful, practical, and thorough guide *Portfolio Teaching: A Guide for Instructors* (available free to users of any Bedford/St. Martin's text), Nedra Reynolds and Rich Rice suggest a series of **conference questions** that will push students to understand their choices and articulate what it is they want to show: progress, independence, creativity. For example,

- Which piece in the working folder deserves the most revision?
- Which piece did classmates enjoy the most?
- Which was the hardest task?
- Which piece makes the research process exciting?
- Which piece causes the most excitement over writing and revising?
- Are there still any unclear assignment requirements?
- How might the portfolio be organized?
- What do you hope will happen?
- Where are the opportunities in the portfolio to make those hopes a reality? (29).

What Should Go into a Portfolio?

As the teacher, you should direct what goes into your students' portfolio, according to the goals of your course. What are your priorities: development of strong paragraphs? Argumentation based on a consistent issue or theme? Mastery of rhetorical modes? Be sure to make students aware of what it is you want them to achieve in the course, and let them know that you will be measuring the portfolio by those standards.

Reynolds and Rice encourage teachers to allow variety in a portfolio's contents, since students have different strengths, are just beginning to explore those differences, and need practice making and presenting informed choices. If the primary text for a course is organized rhetorically, like *Real Skills*, then variety might come through in the different methods of development emphasized in the portfolio essays. However, variety can apply to such things as length, genre, and stages in the writing process. Evaluating such portfolios may be more challenging than if all students' contents were to match tightly drawn archetypes, but this variety can offer "a more complete picture of the student's writing competence" (8).

In a writing course in which five or six pieces of writing are graded, perhaps only two or three of those pieces would typically be included in the portfolio. Teachers who place a strong emphasis on active reading and the integration of reading and writing might also ask students to include one or two annotated assigned readings. Some teachers may want to see some grammar exercises, especially if the student can point out a connection between the work done in grammar and the work done in the essays. Other teachers may encourage students to include writing and images not created for the class but that nevertheless connect in significant ways to the work done in the writing class. What is important is that students learn how to evaluate and select pieces of their work that represent *a meaningful, representative collection.*

Unless a teacher wants only to see "best" work or most recent revisions, then drafts should be represented in the portfolio to validate and document the learning process: for example, marked or graded versions of the essays, plus outlines, drafts, brainstorms, freewrites, reading response sheets, and peer review sheets. If a teacher relies heavily on, say, weekly vignettes or brief write-to-learn pieces to sustain student engagement, then students should have the option to include some of these pieces in their portfolio. Teachers who have pushed students to write in a wide range of styles and situations would likely encourage variety in the portfolio.

Students should also compose a cover letter that discusses the evolution of their writing process across the semester. (See below for more on the cover letter, its importance and possibilities.)

Types of Portfolios

Portfolios can take various forms, again depending on what you, the teacher, want to see. Two common forms are the *process,* or *learning portfolio,* which emphasizes process and a wide variety of evidence of learning, and a *best-works portfolio,* which emphasizes polished revision. And, of course, there are paper, electronic, and Web-based portfolios.

The presentation of the content will depend on the medium. *Paper portfolios* can take a variety of forms. The portfolio might be organized by assignment, with each assignment presented in a cluster together with its drafts and feedback, or as a "narrative," with a cover letter introducing the semester's work from the earliest to the latest days. Some teachers and students prefer a paper presentation for its "archival" qualities—for many, handwriting in particular adds to the personality of the portfolio and provides a clearer sense of its creator.

Electronic portfolios that rely on programs such as Word or PowerPoint offer a practicality and efficiency that may be more appealing to some. Scans of marked work could be introduced or even hotlinked to specific passages for quick reference. If technological literacy has been stressed throughout the course, then an electronic portfolio may be the way to go. An idea-mapping program such as Inspiration can offer creative ways to plan and visualize the presentation.

Web-based (or online) portfolios can offer everything that the aforementioned electronic portfolio can provide, but even more possibilities exist for hyperlinks and wider-world context. Helping students acquire the skills to produce a strong online presence—while becoming better writers, readers, and critical thinkers—could have incredible long-term effects, especially in our media-driven culture. An online course management program such as *WritingClass* (Bedford/St. Martin's), which includes blogs and peer-review tools, lends itself quite nicely to a course integrating online portfolios. Keep in mind, though, that necessary Web-tech skills might prove a barrier for some students, server space needs to be secured, and students, if they are not intimidated by Web creation, can sometimes be tempted to spend more time playing with, say, background colors, images, and hyperlinks than actually revising their essays.

Guiding Student Reflection

Reflecting on Individual Pieces

It is essential that teachers promote critical reflection, for this enables students to articulate what, how, when, and why they are learning. Accordingly, as Reynolds and Rice point out, a portfolio is most effective when students "are invited to collect, select, and reflect on artifacts . . . that best represent their experience and engagement with the learning process" (2). Without reflection, the acts of collection and selection lose meaning, and the portfolio loses shape and rhythm, sagging, as Langston Hughes might say, "like a heavy load" back into undifferentiated storage status.

To help students reflect on individual pieces, you will need to provide guiding questions that correspond with the goals and outcomes listed in your syllabus. In my course, I gave students the following short list of questions to ask themselves after they revised a draft and as they reflected on pieces of writing for inclusion in their portfolios:

QUESTIONS FOR REFLECTING ON A PIECE OF WRITING

- How did my main point (or how I wrote my main point) change?

- What was changed in the introduction? Why was it changed?

- What additional support was needed, and where? Why?

- What additional research was required?

- What is my strongest point or example? How did that change from the draft? Why is it better?

- What was the weakest part of my draft?

- What corrections to grammar, punctuation, and mechanics were necessary? Are these errors I routinely make? How can I improve in these areas?

- Why is the revision better, and why do I care about that?

- What have I learned about writing and revision?

Questions you would use for the same purpose may be very different, depending on your own course goals and the goals of the particular assignment.

The Cover Letter/ Reflective Introduction

The portfolio component that will most clearly synthesize reading, writing, and thinking is the cover letter, sometimes called a reflective introduction. Many teachers, in fact, consider the cover letter the most important document in the portfolio.

Cover letters give portfolio keepers a clear chance to appeal to readers (logos, pathos, ethos), to provide "insider" or "behind-the-scenes" details, and to promote the portfolio's strengths. Some portfolio writers use the cover letter to articulate areas of confusion and goals for future writing and reading. This informs readers that a writer who, for example, has struggled with fused sentences is aware of the struggle, making the error less of a distraction and more of a means of understanding that student's ongoing learning process.

Cover letters, like essays and portfolios, can vary in form, depending on a teacher's guidelines. Length can vary, but many instructors agree that the number of cover letter pages should roughly equal the number of essays or main pieces featured.

That is, a three-page cover letter should provide enough room for students to comment on three main pieces or assignments and to demonstrate self-assessment.

The letter should contain focused, well-structured paragraphs and should point to specific examples from the essays, identified by title, that back the claims the writer makes about his or her progress over the course of the semester. Many cover letters are organized around the pieces of writing included or around course or personal goals. Many effective cover letters also include the following:

- Global and local, or higher-order and lower-order, changes that a student wants readers to notice

- What the portfolio illustrates about the student as writer, reader, and critical thinker

- The struggles the student encountered and what he or she did to overcome them

- Any patterns the student recognizes in his or her learning and writing processes

- Description of specific help given by a writing tutor, a classmate, or the teacher

- A revelatory moment during the course (an "aha!" moment)

- Future writing and reading goals

Note: Students may want to use the cover letter to praise the teacher and the class, and that is fine, if the claims are sincere and are supported with specific reasons and examples. You might want to advise students that overblown praise or claims will come off as insincere, holding back a careful reader or evaluator from embracing the remaining elements of the portfolio. Students may need to be told that the cover letter should not be used to "butter up" a teacher or, say, to appeal for an A.

A sample portfolio assignment follows: from Jim Rice of Quinsigamond Community College. Note that, instead of a cover letter, students are required to write reflective essays on three topics:

1. How you write

2. How you use introductions and conclusions

3. How you would assess your best piece of writing

Sample Portfolio Assignment

The Portfolio's Content

In keeping with the philosophy of portfolio writing, you will write three pieces dealing with three aspects of writing:

- How you write
- How you use introductions and conclusions
- How you would assess your best piece of writing

How You Write

Attach an example of your writing that demonstrates the entire process you use to write a paper.

The supporting materials should include all the work you have done to complete one essay. This may include brainstorming, prewriting, drafting, notes for each revision, peer review, conferences, and the final graded paper.

Your self-assessment should demonstrate your understanding that writing is a process that requires drafting, rewriting, editing, and revision. Write about each of the following categories:

- Clearly **explain** each step you take when writing an essay—from generating the idea and supporting details, through each stage of drafting, up to completion of the final paper.
- Which **one** part of this process did you find most valuable? Why?
- **Quoting** from any of your drafts and any notes you may have, **show** where you made **significant** changes as your essay developed. **Explain** why you made those changes and how they improved the essay. Be sure to point out the significant changes, not superficial changes in spelling and grammar.

Introductions and Conclusions

Take two essays you have written and compare and contrast the introductions and conclusions. Name the type of introduction and compare and/or contrast it with a second selection. Comment on the quality of the introduction, thesis, unity, and support of the introduction. Do the same with the conclusions.

Assess Your Best Piece of Writing

Attach the piece of writing you have done this semester that you consider to be your best work to date. Write persuasively to demonstrate why this sample is your best.

Write about both of the following categories:

- **Identify** three components of good writing. **Explain** why any piece of writing must have these components to ensure reader interest.
- **Quoting** examples from your work, demonstrate how your best work meets the criteria previously identified. **Explain** how your examples achieve what you say they do.

This brief essay should have the following:

- Accurate spelling
- Correct grammar
- Sentence variety
- Proper word usage
- An effective introduction and conclusion
- Thesis
- Paragraphs that have a clear topic sentence, keep to the topic, and progress in a logical order

Assessing the Portfolio

Putting together a successful portfolio takes time and effort: Students need to work hard both writing and critically reflecting on their writing, and you need to provide class time and careful, clear guidance on every step of the process. Assessment is the end game of the long, difficult, but hopefully rewarding process—an attempt to evaluate how successfully both you and your students have done your jobs. Portfolio teaching does not make assessment easier, but it does not make it harder either. Rather, portfolio assessment shifts some of the politics and responsibility of the process. Ultimately, a teacher's guidance is still at the core of the process, but the student has more control over the final product that is assessed. So what kinds of assessment work best with portfolios?

Holistic Evaluation

Provided that you have put the necessary amount of time throughout the semester into helping students become more critical writers and reflective learners, then you need not comment in detail when student work is presented in their final portfolios. This justifies a portfolio being evaluated *holistically*, despite its being comprised of a number of pieces. While it is wonderful at the end of the semester to not annotate in detail or produce substantive comments, it is more wonderful to simply read the portfolios—to become a reader again—and absorb what students have (and have not) learned and what has happened in the class.

Make no mistake: Holistic evaluation is not simply grading from the gut. It requires consistency with the expectations established in the ongoing assessment of student work during the semester and a clear understanding of what was required in the portfolio. Have you clearly guided your students to build upon their reading assignments when composing their essays? Have you set up clear diction-, sentence-, and paragraph-level expectations that enable students to put their exercises into practice in their essays? Then look for evidence of those things in their portfolios. Years of experience in evaluation certainly help, as do conversations with colleagues. (The latter will, of course, be much more formal if portfolio assessment is a departmental requirement or if colleagues assess each other's students' portfolios.)

But how much reflection is enough? Should more have been revised? How can improvement be accurately graded? Well, final evaluation is never simple, but Reynolds and Rice offer three helpful questions to consider when developing a grading guide:

- Do the reflective elements provide reasons for students' choices and identify the changes they have made to essays or projects in preparing the portfolio?

- Are the entries focused, developed, and organized, or do they reflect the qualities of good writing your course has emphasized?

- Is the arrangement and/or navigation scheme effective? (49)

Students should be aware of how important the cover letter will be in your assessment of the whole portfolio. A weak or strong cover letter can be a great illustration of what students have learned in the course. Letters that do not demonstrate metacognition and do not provide specific details, for example, can seriously detract from the strength of a portfolio, even if the essays themselves are quite strong. And letters that take a fresh approach, resisting formula by way of an intriguing metaphor or engaging anecdote, can strengthen the portfolio as a whole. For this reason, you should establish clear guidelines for what you expect in terms of the cover letter's content and style early in the semester.

Remember, though, the key is to look at the whole package. Overall, is the portfolio outstanding, satisfactory, or weak? Do not agonize over a single entry in the portfolio.

This basic rubric (opposite) could help with a holistic assessment of metacognition and writing.

The Question of Grades

For some students and teachers, grading works against learning. For them, grading is, as Erika Lindemann explains in *A Rhetoric for Writing Teachers,* a "destructive judgment valorizing product over process" (220). Many teachers who actually enjoy assessing and commenting on a student's paper resent evaluating it with a letter or number grade (even a high one).

Several legitimate questions arise in discussion of grading the work students do throughout the semester:

- Do grades distract learners from absorbing assessment or motivate them to absorb more?

- Will grades distort a student's selection process when picking pieces to revise for the portfolio (e.g., Why should I pick a paper that already received an A? Or, I am not touching that D paper again), or do grades provide a clearer understanding of what needs to be done?

If grades must be given to individual assignments, according to department requirements, or if a teacher simply wants to give grades, they can be useful—or at least used—when they do not undermine the benefits of process and reflection. In the context of the entire semester's work, most instructors make the finished portfolio count for the most significant percentage of the course grade. Writing submitted earlier in the semester typically carries a significantly lower percentage, because, in the view of most instructors who use portfolios, writers should be evaluated primarily on how their learning has added up during the course, not on their performance at the start of the course. In my opinion, some writing (for example, write-to-learn pieces) should probably never be graded, only commented on. Grades or no grades during the semester, teachers must give students a chance to reflect and learn . . . and reflect again. Portfolios promote this practice.

In the end, whatever assessment methods you choose, you will most likely come to understand why so many of your colleagues are advocates of using portfolios in the writing classroom. After a semester of close work with your students, you will see their learning represented quite clearly in their portfolios. More important, so will they.

Works Cited

Lindemann, Erika. *A Rhetoric for Writing Teachers*. 3rd ed. New York: Oxford UP, 1995. Print.
Reynolds, Nedra, and Rich Rice. *Portfolio Teaching: A Guide for Instructors*. 2nd ed. Boston: Bedford/St. Martin's, 2006. Print.
Zubizarreta, John. *The Learning Portfolio: Reflective Practice for Improving Student Learning*. Bolton: Anker, 2004. Print.

	Cover letter	Thesis statements	Topic sentences	Supporting material	Integration of reading and writing tasks	Explanation and development	Sentence style/complexity	Grammar and mechanics
outstanding								
satisfactory								
weak								

12

Surviving and Growing as a Professional

Unfortunately, many faculty members have neither the training nor the desire to teach developmental students, causing friction within departments. Furthermore, administrative concerns over performance-based funding and student retention can add to faculty frustrations. As teachers of developmental writers, however, we must stand up for their rights as learners. We must also work continually to establish ourselves as respected professionals. Following are (1) an overview of some of the sources of professional and institutional pressure you may encounter on your campus and (2) ideas for managing them. No matter what type of pressure you may feel from your institution, develop a cohesive group within your program and meet each issue with a united front. However, remember that change occurs slowly. Find a couple of colleagues who are committed to improving the developmental writing program, and work together to propose changes.

Admission and Credit Policies

If you are at a community college, your institution probably has an open-door policy. Even though such a policy should guarantee the survival of remediation, that remediation can take various forms. Some experts argue for separate courses that isolate those who need basic skills review or training; other experts push for mainstreaming, which either forces students to learn (or struggle or fail) on their own or requires attendance in a workshop or writing lab. You can find research to back up either approach, so do not think that you must prefer one method or the other. The only true success is that which works at a particular time for a particular student. Those successes will vary from semester to semester, from student to student, and from teacher to teacher. (In fact, if your school requires a common syllabus, make sure that your administration realizes that no matter what the document, it will be interpreted differently by each and every teacher; therefore, even the best-planned ideas will not be carried out uniformly.) Regardless of the form, however, data support the positive effect of developmental programs on both retention and academic performance of entering college students who exhibit deficient skills.

Many experts believe that an ideal class size for developmental courses is around fifteen students. However, few of us are fortunate to teach in a school where this is possible. A more realistic class size to meet administrative approval will be probably around twenty-five. If you find yourself in a seemingly impossible situation, resolve to do the best you can. For instance, if you have, as one teacher did, a total of two hundred students with one section of fifty-four, your main priority will need to be personal survival. One solution is to mark the first couple of papers meticulously. For all other assignments, check only for surface errors and comment only on content and style. If you have access to a writing center, send students there for individual assistance and guidance. For error-filled papers, stop marking surface errors at a certain point. Indicate on the paper where you stopped marking and tell the student what to do next. (For other practical tips on grading papers, see Chapter 10 of this manual.)

Developmental courses are typically relegated to the noncredit realm. Therefore, many students do not feel a sense of obligation to a course that counts neither toward nor against their grade point average nor toward their degree plans. If work in one class must suffer, it will probably be work for your developmental writing class. If students have a test in a credit class, they may decide to skip your class. When they can receive even "elective" credit, they take the course more seriously. Because that is not a possibility in many states, teachers must try to make students realize the personal benefits of remaining in and fully participating in developmental courses. You can offer success stories or testimonials from former students, mention colleagues who prefer students who have successfully completed developmental courses over those straight out of high school, or remind them that the skills they will learn in your course will help them make higher grades in their credit classes without as much effort on their part.

Teaching Assignments

One of the best-kept secrets in academia is the personal satisfaction instructors receive from teaching developmental writers. Because they do not recognize this benefit, many full-time English instructors try to avoid teaching developmental writing classes. Therefore, many departments rely heavily on adjunct instructors and instructors borrowed from other areas, assuming that anyone with a degree can teach a developmental writing class. (Too often, faculty from other disciplines are assigned these courses when enrollment is down in their areas.) In fact, developmental writing students deserve the best and most committed teachers. They need someone who is dedicated and willing to devote lots of energy to helping them learn. Seek out the best teachers and convince them that their skills are needed in the developmental writing classroom. But remember that even some of the best teachers will need training (forums, workshops) in teaching a second dialect or language.

A report about the former Texas Academic Skills Program (TASP)—now THEA—revealed that the quality of developmental education was below professional standards because the majority of teachers in developmental programs lack formal or even informal training in handling these classes effectively. Therefore, they could not implement the most current techniques for teaching underprepared students. (The report also found that faculty in two-year colleges were more likely than faculty in four-year colleges to consider developmental instruction their profession, and that support staff in writing centers, whether in community colleges or universities, generally have a more professional attitude toward developmental education than do members of the faculty.) One solution to this lack of professionalism and training is to encourage attendance at conferences, workshops, and seminars. Perhaps you can even get your administration to fund a guest speaker who will offer advice on reaching the underprepared student. Numerous publications, books, journal articles, and conferences are available to help you become more familiar with developmental writing and thus a better teacher of it. See the bibliography at the end of this chapter for some suggestions.

A different problem can arise when developmental courses are grouped into a separate department away from the college's parallel courses. When placed in their own department, developmental instructors often feel marginalized or segregated from other colleagues because they are not allowed to teach other levels of students. Although this type of arrangement helps the instructor concentrate his or her energies on the developmental writer, it may lead to discouragement. In addition, someone who teaches only developmental courses can lose sight of exceptional writing. We sometimes become excited if we get a paragraph without a major sentence error and forget that style and content are just as important. To maintain perspective, join in departmental and college activities—both professional development and social. Merely having lunch with other instructors can help you refocus on standard communication skills.

If your developmental courses are part of the English department, ask for class assignments that will balance your lower-level courses. For instance, although I did so for years, many of us prefer not to teach first-semester freshman composition while also teaching developmental English. By skipping to at least second-semester courses, you have gained a level of proficiency among the students and given yourself a break from the lower levels. In addition, such skipping can prevent developmental students from following you into their freshman composition classes just because they feel comfortable with you personally. You may discover that you need a break not only from the courses but also from the same students. You could ask for a rotating schedule in which you teach the developmental course every other semester.

If developmental courses are in a separate department, check with the administrators in charge to see if you can teach in both areas. Work closely with both departments; perhaps you could write a proposal suggesting that the two areas be combined or that instructors be allowed to teach in both areas. Point out that both programs will benefit from shared knowledge of students and that the developmental students will receive better preparation for freshman composition and upper-level courses when everyone is working together for the students' best interests.

New adjunct instructors often find themselves in the developmental classroom if full-time teachers do not want to teach the course. If this is your situation, seek out a full-time person to serve as your mentor or guide. Ask questions, and check on departmental guidelines, handouts, and requirements. Exchange information about your classes and your students. You will probably discover that teachers of developmental writing want to share their successes as well as their frustrations. Also, see Chapter 2, Tips for New Instructors, for specific suggestions.

Retention

All good instructors have one major characteristic in common: the desire for all students to succeed. They want students to want to come to class, to enjoy learning, and to leave their classes prepared for other college courses. However, you cannot assume total responsibility for your students' successes or failures. You can make your class as interesting and as relevant as possible; you can offer every student your concern and encouragement, but you cannot make your students attend class or do their homework, and you cannot solve all the personal problems that interfere with their attendance. With declining budgets, administrators often want larger class sizes and seek to hold teachers responsible for students who drop the course. Given the types of students who enroll in developmental courses, some instructors feel a tremendous amount of pressure and a great deal of frustration.

You must remember, and try to get your administration to realize, that open-door students often come to college with health problems, lack of adequate child care, unreliable or nonexistent transportation, inadequate educational backgrounds, and financial problems. And these situations do not disappear just because a student enrolls in college. He or she will continue to have economic, family, and social pressures. Students may enroll in a Monday, Wednesday, Friday class even when they know they do not have a ride to school on Wednesdays. Young students may be under pressure from parents to hold down jobs and earn high grades in college although they never succeeded in high school. In addition, because of their youth, some students are easily swayed by peers to cut class or stay out late. Older students face other difficulties: They have to work overtime, their children's schools take

a holiday, or their children get sick and no baby-sitter is available.

Retention is not just a classroom issue for the instructor. The entire college must become involved. One of the best retention strategies is an orientation. Students need an orientation to the institution, to classes, and to the idea of assessment and placement; they also need to develop a sense of community. Orientation sessions can provide all of that. If your college has an orientation session, find out what kinds of topics are included. If there is no orientation session, propose that the college start offering one. It is amazing that most universities, despite their high standards for admission, provide a week-long orientation for entering students (even longer for foreign students), yet many community colleges, with their open-door policies, do not hold even a single, two-hour session. Orientation should provide reality checks for students. They need information on how to study, read textbooks, take notes, find the support they need, talk with an instructor, and work in groups. Colleges could even use upper-level students to conduct the orientations, an excellent way of helping students meet each other and making the orientation even more meaningful.

Resources for Developmental Professionals

As I mentioned earlier in this chapter, the majority of developmental instructors are not trained to teach developmental courses. Even if you do not have formal training, you can teach yourself (become an active learner) by reading publications in the field and corresponding with others who teach developmental courses. Also, find the money and the time to attend conferences sponsored by professional organizations. Besides the obvious benefits of hearing speakers and obtaining handouts to take back to your own classroom, you can expand your circle of colleagues and learn even more outside the formal sessions. The personal and professional benefits are worth the money, even if you have to pay for the trip (in whole or in part) yourself. In fact, you may get more out of the conference if you are paying the bills.

Too often, developmental instructors fail to take advantage of the resources for professional growth that are available to them. This is hardly surprising, given the institutional pressures described in this chapter, but it creates a vicious circle: If our teaching situations make it impossible for us to connect with other members of our profession—whether by reading what they have said or by meeting up with them at conferences—we miss out on opportunities to improve those very situations.

The following is a brief list of resources you can use to maintain contact with current thinking by other writing instructors. In addition, please get yourself a copy of *Teaching Developmental Writing: Background Readings,* a thoroughly useful collection of professional articles on developmental education compiled by Susan Naomi Bernstein at the University of Cincinnati and offered free of charge to all users of *Real Skills.*

Professional Organizations

Alliance for Computers and Writing (ACW)
ACW is an organization for instructors who want to share practical teaching suggestions regarding the use of technology in the classroom. Contact the Web site for membership information at www.nau.edu/acw/.

College Reading and Learning Association (CRLA)
The CRAL is a group of student-oriented professionals active in the fields of reading, learning assistance, developmental education, and tutorial services at the college/adult level. Membership information can be obtained at the Web site: www.crla.net.

Conference on Basic Writing (CBW)
With a mission to create a network of developmental writing professionals, CBW encourages conversations on pedagogy, curriculum, administration, and social issues affecting developmental writing. Contact the membership Web site at http://orgs.tamu-commerce.edu/CBW/ASU.

National Association for Developmental Education (NADE)
NADE seeks to improve the theory and practice of developmental education in postsecondary education, the professional capabilities of developmental educators, and the design of programs to prepare developmental educators. For more information, contact www.nade.net/.

National Council of Teachers of English (NCTE)
This organization of sixty thousand members is devoted to the improvement of the teaching of English and the language arts at all levels of education. To learn more, check the NCTE Web site: www.ncte.org.

Teachers of English to Speakers of Other Languages (TESOL)
With a membership of eighteen thousand from more than one hundred countries, TESOL seeks to develop expertise and foster communication among teachers teaching English in diverse settings. Search the TESOL Web site: www.tesol.org.

Selected Books

Adler-Kassner, Linda, and Gregory R. Glau. *The Bedford Bibliography for Teachers of Basic Writing.* 2nd ed. Boston: Bedford, 2005. Print.

Bates, Linda, Janet Lane, and Ellen Lange. *Writing Clearly: Responding to ESL Compositions.* Boston: Heinle & Heinle, 1993. Print.

Bernstein, Susan Naomi. *Teaching Developmental Writing: Background Readings.* 3rd ed. Boston: Bedford, 2007. Print.

Enos, Theresa, ed. *A Sourcebook for Basic Writing Teachers.* New York: McGraw, 1987. Print.

Gray-Rosendale, Laura. *Rethinking Basic Writing.* Mahwah: Erlbaum, 2000. Print.

Halasek, Kay, and Nels P. Highberg, eds. *Landmark Essays on Basic Writing.* Mahwah: Erlbaum, 2001. Print.

Harklau, Linda, Kay M. Losey, and Meryl Siegal, eds. *Generation 1.5 Meets College Composition: Issues in the Teaching of Writing to U.S.-Educated Learners of ESL.* Mahwah: Erlbaum, 1999. Print.

Kells, Michelle Hall, and Valerie Balester, eds. *Attending to the Margins: Writing, Researching, and Teaching on the Front Lines.* Portsmouth: Boynton/Cook, 1999. Print.

McNenny, Gerri, and Sallyanne H. Fitzgerald, eds. *Mainstreaming Basic Writers: Politics and Pedagogies of Access.* Mahwah: Erlbaum, 2001. Print.

Rose, Mike. *Lives on the Boundary: A Moving Account of the Struggles and Achievements of America's Educationally Underprepared.* New York: Penguin, 1989. Print.

Shaughnessy, Mina P. *Errors and Expectations: A Guide for the Teaching of Basic Writing.* New York: Oxford UP, 1977. Print.

Selected Journals

College Composition and Communication. 4 issues/year; addresses the concerns of writing specialists, researchers, and teachers of college-level composition courses, through articles on theory, practice, and teaching of composition. NCTE, 1111 West Kenyon Road, Urbana, IL 61801-1096, or (877) 369-6283. To become a subscriber, contact the Web site: www.ncte.org.

College English. 12 issues/year; articles about literature, critical theory, language and applied linguistics, literacy, rhetoric, composition, and professional issues related to the teaching of English. The major publication of the National Council for Teachers of English (NCTE), located at 1111 West Kenyon Road, Urbana, IL 61801-1096; (877) 369-6283. Contact the Web site to become a subscriber: www.ncte.org.

Journal of Basic Writing. 2 issues/year, published with support from the City University of New York. For a subscription, contact the Boyd Printing Company, Inc., attention: Deborah Downing, Subscription Fulfillment, 5 Sand Creek Road, Albany, NY 12205; (518) 436-9686 x134; ddowning@boydprinting.com.

Journal of College Reading and Learning. 2 issues/year; contains theory, research, practice, and policy reflecting the voice of professionals dedicated to postsecondary reading and learning. Contact the Web site to become a subscriber: www.crla.net.

Journal of Developmental Education. 3 issues/year; published by the National Center of Developmental Education, Appalachian State University, Boone, NC 28608. Focuses on research, trends, and news related to postsecondary developmental education. For subscription information, visit www.ncde .appstate.edu/jde.htm.

Teachers of English to Speakers of Other Languages (TESOL) Quarterly. 4 issues/year; bridges theory and practice for teachers, researchers, and scholars in linguistic disciplines. To subscribe, contact www.tesol.org.

Teaching English in the Two-Year College (TETYC). 4 issues/year; for the two-year college English teacher as well as for freshman and sophomore composition teachers in four-year schools; focuses on the teaching of composition. NCTE, 1111 West Kenyon Road, Urbana, IL 61801-1096, or (877) 369-6283. Contact the Web site to become a subscriber: www.ncte.org.

Selected Web Sites

Clearinghouse on Reading, English, and Communication
http://reading.indiana.edu
This site allows customized searches of news, lesson plans, Web resources, and other materials related to reading, English, and communication.

The Epiphany Project www.has.vcu.edu/epiphany/
The Epiphany Project provides strategies and support to assist mainstream writing faculty with integrating technology into their classrooms.

National Association for Developmental Education (NADE) www.nade.net
This forum is intended to improve the theory and practice of developmental education. Links include collaborative learning and computer-based instruction.

National Council for Teachers of English (NCTE)
www.ncte.org
NCTE's mission is the advancement of the teaching of English and language arts at all levels of education. This Web site has links to relevant resources.

Re: Writing
bedfordstmartins.com/rewriting
This site includes online workshops, bibliographies, and journals for professional development. *Re: Writing* provides access to *The Bedford Bibliography for Teachers of*

Basic Writing, an annotated list of books, articles, and periodicals.

Teachers of English to Speakers of Other Languages (TESOL) www.tesol.org
TESOL's mission is to develop expertise in teaching English to speakers of other languages. This Web site offers links to education programs and publications.

Selected Listservs

A listserv is an e-mail discussion group. Each listserv has two addresses: One is the administrative address, and the other is the discussion address. The administrative address provides access to information about the list, whereas the other address is for the discussion itself; you will receive this address once you subscribe to the listserv, and any messages you send to that location will reach everyone on the list.

The addresses listed below are the administrative locations for each listserv. If you would like a fuller explanation of what subject matter a particular listserv covers, e-mail the administrator with the command "INFO [name of listserv]" in the subject line or message. Often, the administrator will specify a procedure for subscribing to the listserv, should you choose to do so. If such information is not provided, you can e-mail the administrator with the command "SUBSCRIBE [name of listserv] [your first name, your last name]." (Try this first, and if it fails to work, substitute your e-mail address for your name.) Finally, having subscribed to the list, you will first receive a Frequently Asked Questions (FAQ) file, which will have important information about how the listserv operates.

AEDNET: Adult Education Discussion
listserv@alpha.acast.nova.edu

CBW-L: Conference on Basic Writing
listserv@umn.edu

ECOMP-L: College English Composition
listserv@listserv.nodak.edu

LRNASST-L: Learning Assistance Listserv
listserv@lists.ufl.edu

MULTC-ED: Multicultural Education Discussion
listserv@umdd.umd.edu

NCTE listservs
To subscribe, visit www.ncte.org

Student Paper Submission Form

Instructors: Please use duplicates of this form for each piece of student writing that you submit for possible publication in future editions of *Real Skills, Real Writing,* or *Real Essays* by Susan Anker. In order to get permission from, and pay, students whose papers we decide to publish, it is very important that we know how to contact them. With that in mind, please make sure to include students' addresses and phone numbers.

Please submit the completed form(s) and paper(s) to:

Anker Paper Submissions
Bedford/St. Martin's
75 Arlington Street, 8th Floor
Boston, MA 02116

For each student paragraph or essay that we publish in future editions of *Real Skills, Real Writing,* or *Real Essays* we will pay you and the student each $100.

Information about you:

Instructor's Name _____ Title _____

Department _____ Office phone _____
                                                     (area code)
School _____

Mailing address _____
        (city)   (state)   (zip code)

E-mail address _____

Information about the paper you are submitting:

Student's name _____

Student's address _____
            (city)   (state)   (zip code)

Student's phone number _____
                (area code)

E-mail address _____

Title of the paper _____

Assignment for which the paper was written: _____

_____

_____